CHINESE DIMSUM RECIPES

WEATHERVANE BOOKS
New York

PUBLISHED 1985 BY WEATHERVANE
BOOKS, DISTRIBUTED BY CROWN
PUBLISHERS, INC.
PRINTED IN TAIPEI, TAIWAN, REPUBLIC OF CHINA
ISBN 0-517-475111
h g f e d c b a

FOREWORD

Most Western desserts are very fattening. For people who are overweight and people who have heart disease, those desserts are taboos.

The utensils used to make Western desserts are complicated. The Chinese way of making desserts is different. Though we do not have various kinds of utensils, we can still make various kinds of delicious desserts with simple ingredients.

Many housewives are troubled by the method of preparing dough for different kinds of pastries. They do not know how much flour to use for the number of servings.

This book offers simple methods to solve these problems. We introduce 109 recipes for Chinese pastries and desserts. You will find them easy to make, money-saving, and tasty.

CHINESE DIMSUM RECIPES

CONTENTS:

2. Rice 66-67

3. Assorted

4. Cold Desserts 114-115

Notes:

1. Unless otherwise specified, each recipe serves 4 to 6.
2. The English title of this book is Chinese Dimsum Recipes because the Chinese call snacks and desserts dimsum or dien-hsin.
3. There are three kinds of flour mentioned in this book, the all-purpose flour, the plain wheat flour, and the cake flour. The difference among them is that all-purpose flour is the richest in protein and the cake flour has the smallest amount of protein. This is why pastries made from all-purpose flour are more elastic then those made from plain wheat flour; and pastries made from plain wheat flour are more elastic than those made from cake flour. To get the best result, we suggest you use the flour we name in each recipe. Or you can use all-purpose flour if other kinds of flour are not available.

麵食類

Noodles and Watered Dough

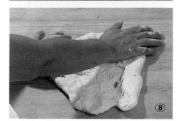

How to make dough

1. (A) No matter fluid or solid a dough may be, the average amount of flour to use is about 1/2 cup per person —for example, use 2 cups of flour for 4 people. Of course, this is subject to change according to the appetite of the people who are going to be served.

   (B) After measureing, sift flour carefully into a large container. If it for leavened dough, sift three times to make sure that the flour mixes well with the other ingredients.

2. Make a well in the middle. Add water to it slowly, stirring with a fork or chopsticks. You can put 1 tablespoon of lard in to make the dough smooth and shiny.

3. Keep adding water till the flour turns into small lumps.

4. Flour your hands lightly. What follow is hand work.

5. Hand work is the literal meaning of kneading and rubbing the lumps into a dough.

6. Soak a piece of clean gauze or cheesecloth in water, then wring it dry.

7. Cover the dough with the wet gauze. Let stand for 20-25 minutes. This step is called Hsing-Mein, or "to let the dough wake up." The purpose is to let the flour become completely moistened by the water.

8. If you want the pastries to be very elastic, remember to apply the hand work of kneading, pulling, and pushing, whether it is a leavened or scalded dough.

9. If you don't want your pastries to be very elastic, apply the method of pressing and cutting as frequently as possible.

10. The longer you Knead, pull, and press, the smoother and tenderer the pastry dough will be. Otherwise, it will feel grainy and rough.

11. If you are a greenhorn at making food with flour, adding the correct amount of water might be a problem. If the dough is too wet to knead, just put some flour to one side and add little by little while kneading till the dough is moderately soft.

12. If the dough is too dry and is hard to knead, just cut it open or make some cuts on it, sprinkle on some water, and knead. Repeat till the dough is firm enough.

13. Keep kneading the dough till very smooth; then you can start making pastries. If you are not in a hurry to do so, just cover it iwth a piece of wet cloth.

Notes:

1. Generally speaking, the ideal proportion of water to flour is 1 to 3.

2. Beaten egg can replace some of the water to make the pastry more nutritious.

Chicken E-Mein Soup

Ingredients:
2 chicken legs, 4^1/$_2$ cups cold water, 1 tablespoon ginger wine, 10 ounces E-Mein
(I) 1^1/$_2$ teaspoons salt, ^{1}/$_2$ teaspoon MSG
Method:
1. Wash the chicken legs and cut into 1-inch pieces. Cook in boiling water for 1 minute and remove to a casserole bowl. Add cold water and ginger wine. Put in a steamer to steam for 40 minutes. Remove and add ingredients (I).
2. Cook E-Mein in boiling water for ^{1}/$_2$ minute and drain. Put E-Mein in chicken soup.

Bean Noodles Broth

Ingredients:
1^1/$_2$ ounces dried lily flowers, 4 tablespoons sliced fish stock, 4 coils Chinese bean noodles
(I) 8 cups cold soup stock, 2 tablespoons cornstarch
(II) 1/3 cup shredded black mushrooms, ^{1}/$_4$ cup shredded lean pork, ^{1}/$_4$ cup shredded bamboo shoot
(III) 1 tablespoon soy sauce, 2 teaspoons salt, ^{1}/$_2$ tablespoon sugar, ^{1}/$_2$ teaspoon MSG
(IV) 2 tablespoons chopped parsley and scallion, some sesame oil
Method:
1. Remove footstalks from dried lily flowers. Soak in water for about 10 minutes. Drain.
2. Blend ingredient (I) well. Bring to a boil over medium heat. Add the lily flowers, sliced fish stock, and ingredients (II) and return to a boil.
3. Put in Chinese bean noodles and ingredients (III). Use chopsticks to loose the noodles. Sprinkle ingredients (IV) on soup. Take off the heat and serve.
Notes:
1. Chinese bean noodles are made from bean starch. They are available in Oriental markets.
2. You can use instead E-Fu-Mein, which is steamed, then fried.

Homemade Bean Threads

Ingredients:
5 ounces green bean starch, 16 ounces rice flour, 4 tablespoons oil, 3 tablespoons sliced scallions, 8 cups soup stock
(I) ^{1}/$_3$ cup shredded pork, ^{1}/$_4$ cup shredded squid (soaked), ^{1}/$_4$ cup shredded fungus, ^{1}/$_4$ cup shredded green vegetable, ^{1}/$_4$ cup shredded bamboo shoot
(II) 1^1/$_2$ teaspoons salt, 1 tablespoon soy sauce, ^{1}/$_2$ teaspoon MSG, 1 teaspoon sherry.
Method:
1. Mix green bean starch thoroughly with rice flour. Add enough water to make a thick paste.
2. Grease a skillet thoroughly. Pour in the paste and shake the skillet to spread the mixture in a thin layer. Cook over low to medium heat, turning it over to cook on both sides. Do not let it get scorched. Remove and let cool. Cut into long threads.
3. Pour oil into a frying pan. Stir-fry the sliced scallion briefly, add ingredients (I) and (II) and continue to stir-fry. Add the stock and bring to a boil. Put in the green bean threads to cook for another 3 minutes. Remove and serve.
Notes:
1. Pepper, parsley and red chili pepper can be added freely.
2. Another way to cook green bean threads is by boiling. Or you can stuff green bean wrappers with a filling and deep-fry them.

牛肉湯刀削麵
Tao-Hsiao-Mein in Beef Brisket Soup

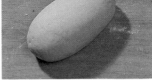

Ingredients:

1¹/₄ pounds beef brisket, 3 cups plain wheat flour

(I) 1 slice ginger, 1 scallion (sliced), ¹/₂ tablespoon aniseed, ¹/₂ tablespoon cumin, 1 mangosteen, 3 tablespoons sherry, 1 teaspoon salt

(II) 2 tablespoons chopped scallion, 1 tablespoon parsley, ¹/₂ teaspoon MSG, ¹/₂ teaspoon pepper

Method:

1. Wash the beef and cut into 1-inch cubes. Cook in boiling water to cover for 1 minute. Remove and rinse.
2. Wrap the spices in ingredients (I) in a piece of cheese cloth. Bring 15 cups of water, the brisket, salt, sherry, and the spice bag to a boil. Turn the heat down to low and simmer till the beef is well cooked. Discard the spice bag. Reserve the rest.
3. Knead flour with enough water to make a stiff dough. Cover the dough with a piece of wet cloth and let rest for 20 minutes. Knead again till it is very smooth. Shape it into a long, rounded pillow.
4. Bring a pot of water to a boil. Add 1¹/₂ teaspoons salt. Holding the dough in one hand, slice it with a knife into ribbonlike noodles about ¹/₃" wide. Cook the noodles in boiling water for 1 minutes. Ladle out and put in the beef soup. Bring it to a boil and cook for another 2-3 minutes. Remove and serve, sprinkled with ingredients (II).

Note:

Be sure to make your dough a little stiff and dry so it will be easy to be cut and more elastic to eat.

辣肉醬炒通心粉
Pork Sauce Macaroni

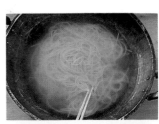

Ingredients:

1 pound macaroni, 4 tablespoons oil, sliced cucumber, onion rings

(I) 8 ounces lean ground pork, 1 tablespoon hot bean paste, 2 teaspoons chopped chili pepper, 1 cup soup stock

(II) 1 teaspoon salt, 1 teaspoon sugar, ¹/₂ tablespoon ginger wine, 1 tablespoon chopped scallion, ¹/₂ teaspoon MSG

Method:

1. Bring a pot of water to a boil and add 1 teaspoon salt. Put in the macaroni and cook for 7-8 minutes. Drain and rinse under cold running water.
2. Put oil in a frying pan. Stir-fry ingredients (I) and (II) till it all smells good. Add the macaroni and stir-fry till evenly mixed. Remove.
3. Garnish with cucumber slices and onion rings.

Notes:

1. You can choose the type of macaroni you like, since various kinds are suitable.
2. Another way of cooking macaroni is to bake boiled macaroni with greated cheese and sauce on top.

海鮮烏龍麵
Wu-Lung Noodles in Seafood Soup

Ingredients:

5 ounces shrimps (shelled), 1 sea crab, 1 squid head (soaked), some dried black mushrooms, 1 sea cucumber, 8 clams, 4 ounce lean pork, 6 cups soup stock, 3 tablespoons sliced stock fish, 4 quail eggs, 4 packs of Wu-Lung noodles

(I) 1 teaspoon salt, 1 tablespoon ginger wine, $1/2$ teaspoon pepper

Method:

1. Wash the shrimps, remove the intestine, and rinse. Rinse the crab and cut into pieces. Rinse the squid and cut into 1" pieces. Trim footstalks from dried black mushrooms and soak in water. Rinse the sea cucumber and slice it. Open the clams with a knife and rinse. Slice the pork.

2. Put the soup stock in a saucepan. Add the stock fish, pork, black mushrooms, quail eggs, and sea cucumber. Bring to a boil, add the noodles, crab, and ingredients (I) and boil for 2 minutes. Add the shrimps, squid, and clams. Boil briefly and serve.

Note:

Remove any scum from the surface during cooking.

麻油鷄麵線
Mein-Hsien (Thin Noodles) in Sesame Oil Chicken Soup

Ingredients:

4 chicken legs, 4 ginger slices, 1 bundle of mein-hsien, 6 tablespoons black sesame oil, 2 tablespoons rice wine, 6 cups water

Method:

1. Rinse the chicken legs and cut each into 4 pieces.
2. Cut the mein-hsien with scissors into long sections. Put on a piece of clean cloth. Puth the cloth on a plate. Bring a cup of water in a steamer to a boil. Steam the mein-hsien for 2 minutes.
3. Put sesame oil in a frying pan. Fry the ginger for a while, add the chicken pieces, and stir-fry till the color changes. Add the wine and water. Bring to a boil and add the mein-hsien. When soup returns to a boil, serve.

Note:

Leave the mein-hsien in the steamer until you want to stir-fry it. Rinse it gently before cooking.

台式炒油麵
Chow-Yiu-Mein, Taiwanese Style

Ingredients:
2 cups plain wheat flour, 1/4 cup all-purpose flour, 1 teaspoon baking soda, 1 1/2 cups water, 5 ounces bean sprouts, 10 ounces fresh oysters (without shells), 4 tablespoons cornstarch, 3 tablespoons sliced scallion, 4 tablespoons oil, 1/2 cup shredded pork, 1/2 cup shredded Chinese Cabbage

Seasonings:
1 tablespoon ginger juice, 1/3 teaspoon five-spice powder, 1 1/2 teaspoons salt, 1 tablespoon soy sauce, 1/2 teaspoon MSG, 1/2 teaspoon pepper, 1/2 teaspoon sherry, 1/2 cup soup stock.

Method:
1. Sift the flours together. Dissolve the baking soda in the water and knead into the flour to make a yellowish dough. Let it stand for 20-25 minutes. Use a noodle maker to make the dough into yiu-mein (oiled noodles).
2. Cook the noodles in boiling water for 1-2 minutes. Drain and blend in a tablespoon of oil.
3. Trim root parts from the bean sprouts, rinse, and drain. Wash the oysters with water mixed with a little salt. Pick out any impurities. Rinse off the salted water under running water. Drain. Add cornstarch to the oysters. Mix well.
4. Bring a pot of water to a boil. Add the oysters and cook for 1/2 minute. Romove and rinse with cold water.
5. Pour oil into a frying pan. Stir-fry the sliced scallion till it smells good. Add the pork and stir-fry till the color changes. Add the shredded Chinese cabbage and stir-fry till softened. Put in bean sprouts, yiu-mein, and seasonings. Stir-fry briefly. Simmer, covered for 1 minute. Remove the cover, stir-fry briefly, and serve.

Note:
This can be made with leftover yiu-mein.

陽春麵
Yang-Chun-Mein

Ingredients:
1 teaspoon salt, 16 ounces green vegetable
(I) 2 cups plain wheat flour (or 16 ounces machine-made noodles)
(II) 10 ounces pig's bones, 1 1/2 ounces small scallops, 10 ounces chicken feet, 1 slice of ginger, 1 scallion (sliced), 1 tablespoon sherry, 1/2 teaspoon salt, 1/2 teaspoon MSG, 12 cups water

Method:
1. Wash the pig's bones. Soak the scalops in water for a while, then brush off any sand. Soak in water again for 4 hours. Remove and crush. Wash the chicken feet. Cut each into 2 pieces.
2. Put ingredients (II) except MSG in a pot. Boil till liquid is reduced by a third. Add the MSG, then turn off the heat. Strain the liquid into a clean bowl.
3. Mix the flour with some water and knead into a dough. Press it flat with a noodle machine or roll it into a large flat piece. Cut the piece into noodles.
4. Bring a large pot of water to a boil. Add the salt, then the noodles. Boil for 1 minute. Remove to a serving bowl and pour in the broth.
5. Rinse the green vegetable, trim off old and withered parts, and cut into pieces. Boil in water and put on top of the noodles.

Notes:
1. When making this dish, remember to make more soup and less noodles.
2. Machine-made noodles are very soft and easily cooked. They are suitable for children and people with digestive ailments.

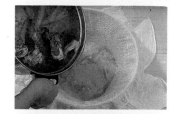

雜醬拌麵

La-Mein in Special Sauce

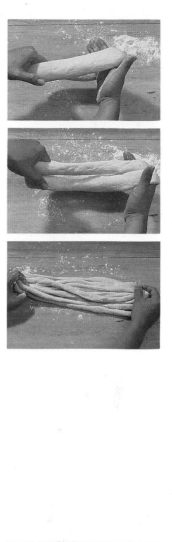

Ingredients:
cold boiled water, 5 tablespoons oil
(I) $2^1/2$ cups all-purpose flour, $1/4$ cup cake flour, water (about 104°F) (or $1^1/3$ pounds ready-made la-mein)
(II) 2 tablespoons broad bean paste, 2 tablespoons sweet bean sauce, $1/2$ tablespoon soy sauce, $1^1/2$ tablespoons chopped scallion, $1/2$ tablespoon sugar, $1/2$ teaspoon MSG, 5 ounces water
(III) 8 ounces diced pork, 3 tablespoons diced cucumber, 3 tablespoons diced carrot, 4 tablespoons diced salted vegetable root, 4 tablespoons diced bamboo shoot
(IV) 2 tablespoons peanut oil or sesame oil

Method:
1. Mix the two kinds of flour together. Knead with enough warm water to make a soft dough. Cover with a piece of wet cloth and let stand for 20 minutes. Knead again thoroughly to make the dough elastic.
2. Lightly flour the dough. Shape it into a long roll. Wind the roll around two rolling pins. Pull apart slowly from opposite directions. The distance between the two rolling pins depends on your strength. Let it go slack. Wind around and pull again. Keep winding and pulling till the roll becomes threads. Remember to flour the roll every time before you wind and pull. (There is a labor-saving way to make la-mein: Fix one rolling pin so it doesn't move, and pull out the dough with the other rolling pin.)
3. Bring a pot of water to a boil and cook the la-mein for 1-2 minutes. Add a little cold water and bring to a boil again. Ladle out and soak in cold boiled water till cool. (In winter, this step can be omitted.) Drain. Blend well with ingredient (IV).
4. Pour oil into a frying pan. Stir-fry the mixed ingredients (II) first till it all smells good. Add ingredients (III) and cook for 3 minutes. Remove and blend with la-mein. Serve.

Notes:
1. Other kinds of noodles can be used to replace la-mein.
2. In summer, after blending the la-mein with oil, you can refrigerate it. Blend with some sauce before serving.
3. If you want to make sure that the noodles are cooked, pick up one thread, break it, and examine the cross section. If it is white in the center and transparent around, the noodle is done.
4. If you like a strong taste, increase the amount of seasoning or add $1/2$ teaspoon of chopped chili pepper.

打滷麵

Ta-Lu Mein

Ingredients:
8 ounces pork, 3 ounces fungus, 6 tablespoons oil, $1/2$ tablespoon chopped scallion and garlic stem, 10 slices carrot, 10 large cucumber slices, 8 cups clear broth (made from pig's bones), 2 tablespoons cornstarch paste, 2 eggs (well beaten), 16 ounces noodles (la-mein, chieh-mein, or tao-hsiao-mein)

Seasoning:
(I) $1^1/2$ tablespoons soy sauce, 1 teaspoon salt, $1/2$ teaspoon MSG
(II) 3 tablespoons sesame oil, $1^1/2$ teaspoons pepper

Method:
1. Cut the pork into big, thin slices. Rinse the fungus and cut into 1" squares.
2. Put oil in a large frying pan. Stir-fry the chopped scallion and garlic stem till they smell good. Add the sliced ingredients. Add seasoning (I) while stir-frying; $1^1/2$ minutes later, pour in the clear broth. Bring to a boil. Add the cornstarch paste slowly to make the soup creamy. Turn off the heat. When the soup cools down a little bit, pour in the egg batter and stir-slightly.
3. Bring a pot of water to a boil. Add the noodles. When cooked, ladle out the noodles and place in a soup bowl. Pour in the creamy soup. Sprinkle with seasoning (II). Serve.

Note:
La-mein are the noodles pulled into strips from dough. Chien-mein are like vermicelli, freshly made and cut with a knife. Tao-hsiao-mein are ribbonlike noodles cut with knife.

廣式炒麵

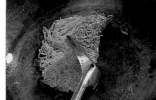

Chow-Mein, Cantonese Style

Ingredients:
5 eggs, 2^1/2 cups plain wheat flour, 2/3 cup oil, 10 ounces green-stemmed flat cabbage, several dark mushrooms, 8 ounces cha-shao-jou (barbecued pork), 1 ounce shelled shrimps, 5 ounces oiled chicken, 5 ounces roasted duck, 10 slices of cucumber, several slices of bamboo shoot, several quail eggs, 1 tablespoon sherry

Seasoning:
(I)   MSG, 1^1/2 teaspoons salt, ^{1}/2 teaspoon white pepper
(II) ^{1}/2 teaspoon salt, 1/3 teaspoon MSG, ^{1}/2 teaspoon soy sauce, 2 tablespoons cornstarch
      paste, 1/3 cup soup stock or water

Method:
1. Beat the eggs lightly; there shouldn't be too many bubbles. Mix slowly with flour. Knead to a dough. Cut the dough into noodles with a noodle machine.
2. Bring a pot of water to a boil. Cook the noodles till half done. Ladle cut and soak in cold water till cool. Drain. Blend evenly with 2 tablespoons of oil.
3. Rinse cabbage, remove old and withered stems and leaves, and cut into 2"×1/3" strips. Rinse the mushrooms and cut into wide shreds.
4. Grease a large frying pan with 6 tablespoons of oil. Put in the noodles and stir to loosen with chopsticks. Put in seasoning (I) and stir-fry thoroughly. Coil the noodles. Add 4 table-spoons of oil slowly along the rim. Cover and fry (not stir-fry) till the noodles become brown-ed. Shake the pan. When the noodles no longer stick to the bottom, turn the other side up. Add another 4 tablespoons of oil, as before. Fry till a little scorched. Remove to a serving plate. Keep the remaining oil in the pan.
5. Put the barbecued pork, cabbage, mushrooms, shrimps, oiled chicken, roasted duck, cucumber slices, bamboo shoot slices, shelled quail eggs, and seasoning (II) in the pan and stir-fry for 1 minute. Sprinkle with sherry. Turn off the heat.
6. Put the stir-fried mixture on the noodles. Serve.

Notes:
1. In Cantonese style, the noodles have to be fried till both sides are browned.
2. Egg noodles are crispy and delicious, but require more oil.
3. If you choose the ready-made E-Fu noodles, use following cooking method: Put 4 tablespoons of oil in a large frying pan. Stir-fry scallion and garlic stem till they smell good. Add green-stemmed flat cabbage and mushrooms. Stir-fry briefly. Pour in a cup of soup stock, salt, soy sauce, and coiled noodles. Simmer, covered. When the soup is boiling, add the barbecued pork and MSG, then pour in the cornstarch paste. Bring to a boil again and serve.
4. Cha-shao-jou, oiled chicken and roasted duck are all cooked items which can be bought in Cantonese restaurants.

咖哩牛肉炒麵

Curry Beef Chow-Mein

Ingredients:
10 ounces spinach, 1^1/2 teaspoons salt, 3 cups plain wheat flour, 10 ounces beef, 6 table-spoons oil, 1 large onion (sliced into 1" pieces), 1^1/2 cups soup stock, 3 ounces snow peas (trimmed)
(I)   1 tablespon cornstarch, ^{1}/2 egg white, 1 tablespoon ginger wine
(II) 4 tablespoons chopped red scallion head, 1 tablespoon chopped ginger and garlic
(III) 5 tablespoons curry powder, ^{1}/2 cup milk, ^{1}/2 teaspoon salt, 1^1/2 tablespoons sugar

Method:
1. Remove old and withered stems and leaves from the spinach. Pick out about 2 ounces of tender leaves to mince. Rub the rest with salt in a basin till the green juice oozes out.
2. Blend the minced spinach with the green juice. Knead into the flour to make a green dough. Add water if necessary. Cut the dough into noodles with a noodle machine, or you can roll out the dough to a big, thin piece, flour the surface, fold it into a 5"-wide strip, then cut into noodles with a knife.
3. Rinse the beef and cut into 1" cubes. Marinate with ingredients (I) for 20 minutes.
4. Bring water to a boil. Boil the noodles for 1^1/2 minutes. Drain.
5. Put oil in a frying pan. Fry ingredients (II) for a while. Add the onion and ingredients (III), then the beef slices. Stir-fry till the color of the beef changes. Add the noodles and soup stock. Let boil for 2 minutes. Add the snow peas. Stir-fry for 1 minute and serve.

Note:
Red scallion head is the root parts of a kind of scallions which are red on the surface.

溫州大餛飩

Wonton, Wenchou Style

Ingredients:
5 ounces shelled shrimps, 5 ounces lean ground pork, 6 tablespoons chopped green-stemmed vegetable, 4 tablespoons diced spiced bean curd, 4 tablespoons diced egg pancake, 10 ounces thick wonton skins (or 8 ounces thin ones), $8^{1}/_{2}$ cups soup stock (mixed with 1 teaspoon salt), 6-8 tung-hao or spinach.

(I) 1 teaspoon salt, 1/3 teaspoon MSG, $^{1}/_{4}$ teaspoon white pepper, $^{1}/_{2}$ tablespoon ginger wine

(II) 1/3 cup shredded salted vegetable root, 1/3 cup shredded laver, 1/3 cup shredded egg pancake, 1/3 cup chopped scallions

Method:

1. (A) Shrimp and pork filling:
   Rinse the shrimps, drain, mince with the ground pork, and blend well with ingredients (I).

   (B) Pork and vegetable filling:
   Sprinkle salt on the chopped green-stemmed vegetable, squeeze dry, mince with the ground pork, add the diced spiced bean curd and egg pancake, and blend well with all of ingredients (I) except the ginger wine.

   (C) Vegetable filling:
   Use the ingredients in filling (B) except ground pork. Add 2 teaspoons of sesame oil and $1^{1}/_{2}$ teaspoons of sugar.

2. Spread $^{1}/_{2}$ tablespoon filling on a wonton skin and pinch the four corners together gently; or place filling on one corner, fold the skin up to make a triangle, then pinch together the two outer corners; or fold into a square pillow shape (mostly for the one with vegetable filling).

3. Bring soup stock to a boil. Add the wontons and boil for 1 minute. Put in tung-hao or spinach (which has been washed cleen and torn into 1" pieces). Cook briefly and serve.

4. Add ingredients (II), sesame oil, and pepper to increase the flavor.

Notes:

1. There are big wonton skin and small ones. The former are used in this dish.

2. To make egg pancake, beat eggs till smooth. Heat oil in a large frying pan (do not let it get too hot). Pour the egg batter in gently so that it forms a thin layer in the pan. It is done when no longer runny.

花生石頭餅

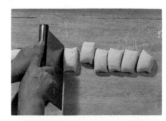

Peanut-Flavored Stone Biscuit

Ingredients:
2 cups plain wheat flour, $^{3}/_{4}$ cup cake flour, 3 tablespoons sugar, $^{1}/_{2}$ teaspoon salt, $^{1}/_{2}$ cup peanut powder

Method:

1. Blend the ingredients well. Mix with enough water to make a hard dough.

2. Spread stones in a large frying pan. Heat over high heat. When stones are hot enough to immediately vaporize water sprinkled on them, reduce the heat to medium.

3. Divide the dough into several parts and roll out each to a circle. Place one by one on the hot stones. Bake till crisp and hard. (Do not turn.) Remove and let cool on a wire rack.

Note:
While making stone biscuits, you can bland stir-fried flour with uncooked flour or use peanut powder or sesame powder instead, as you like.

Cat's Ears

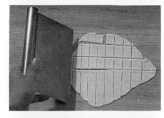

Ingredients:

1³/₄ cups plain wheat flour, ¹/₂ teaspoon salt, 6 tablespoons shelled shrimps, 2 teaspoons cornstarch, 10 ounces spinach, 4 tablespoons oil, 6 tablespoons sliced lean pork,
8 cups soup stock

(I) 4 tablespoons sliced fungus, 6 tablespoons sliced fresh squid

(II) 2 teaspoons salt, ¹/₂ teaspoon MSG, 1¹/₂ teaspoons ginger wine

Method:

1. Knead the flour with salt and enough water to make a dough. Let stand for 20
   minutes. Knead again till very smooth. Divide into 3 or 4 parts.

2. Roll each part into a long strip, then cut into 1" squares. Pinch each square into
   the shape of a cat's ear.

3. Rinse the shrimps and drain. Add cornstarch and blend well. Remove old and
   withered parts from the spinach, wash, and cut into 1"-wide strips.

4. Pour oil into a frying pan. Put in the sliced pork and stir-fry till it smells good.
   Add the stock and bring to a boil. Put in the cat's ears and boil for another 2 minutes.
   Add ingredients (I) and (II) and the shrimps and spinach. Bring to a boil and serve.

Note:

You can alter the soup ingredients as you wish.

Flour-Fish Soup

Ingredients:

4 tablespoons oil, 9 cups soup stock, ¹/₄ cup shredded carrot, 2 cups shredded
green-stemmed flat cabbage

(I) 2 cups plain wheat flour, 1/3 teaspoon salt

(II) ¹/₄ cup shredded pork, ¹/₄ cup shredded bamboo shoot, 2 tablespoons shredded scallion

Seasoning:

(I) 1¹/₂ teaspoons salt, ¹/₂ teaspoon MSG, 1 tablespoon soy sauce

(II) ¹/₂ teaspoon pepper, 1 tablespoon sesame oil

Method:

1. Mix ingredients (I) with enough water to make a bowl of paste. Let stand for 15
   minutes. Blend again thoroughly to make the paste smooth and grainless.

2. Put oil in a large frying pan. Stir-fry ingredients (II) till they smell good. Add the
   stock and shredded carrot. Bring to a boil.

3. Tilt the bowl of paste slightly and use a chopstick to put the paste in the boiling
   soup, bit by bit. When the slices pile up in the pan, separate them with a spatula.
   After all the slices are in the pan, add the shredded cabbage and seasoning (I).
   Boil for another 2 minutes. Remove and serve.

4. Sprinkle seasoning (II) on top.

Note:

You can add eggs into the paste to make it more nutritious, it will be less elastic in texture.

蘿蔔絲餅

Cake of Turnip Shreds

Ingredients:

3 cups plain wheat flour, 4 tablespoons dried baby shrimps, 1¹/₂ cups shredded turnip, 2 garlic stems, 2 tablespoons oil, 4 tablespoons chopped pork, 1 cup oil, tablespoon cornstarch paste

(I) 1 teaspoon salt, 1 teaspoon sugar

(II) 1 teaspoon salt, ¹/₂ teaspoon pepper, ¹/₂ teaspoon MSG

Method:

1. Knead enough water into the flour to make a moderately soft dough. Divide into 8-10 pieces.
2. Rinse the shrimps and soak in water for 10 minutes. Chop. Blend shredded turnip with ingredients (I) and let stand for 20 minutes. Squeeze dry. Slice the garlic on a slant.
3. Pour 2 tablespoons oil into a frying pan. Stir-fry the shrimps and chopped pork till they smell good. Add shredded turnip, garlic, and ingredients (II). Stir-fry well. Add cornstarch paste to thicken. (The mixture should be sticky.) Remove. Divide into 8-10 parts.
4. Roll each dough piece into a thin pancake. Place filling in the center of each pancake and wrap up. Shape into patties.
5. Pour 1 cup of oil into frying pan. Heat to over medium-hot, lower the heat, and place the patties in the pan. Cook, turning once, until the crust becomes browned and slightly scorched.

Notes:

1. You can skip the step of stir-frying and just blend cornstarch with raw ingredients for filling.
2. You can use Chinese cabbage and bottle gourd to replace the turnip.

鮮奶餅

Milk Pancakes

Ingredients:

1¹/₂ cups milk, ¹/₂ cup sugar, 2 cups plain wheat flour, 1 tablespoon butter

Method:

1. Put the milk and sugar in a small saucepan. Heat, stirring, over a low flame to melt the sugar. Add the flour and stir to a smooth paste. Let stand for 20 minutes. Blend again.
2. Grease a frying pan with butter. Follow with either of the two steps below.
   (A) Heat the pan. Put in a tablespoon of the batter. Shake the pan so the batter swirls into a circle. Bake over low heat. When the batter is no longer runny, remove. Serve by itself or with jam.
   (B) Heat the pan. Add the batter and shake the pan as above. Bake over low heat. When the pancake is still soft but no longer runny, turn and cook on the other side. Remove. Roll it up to eat.

Note:

If you do not like sweet food, use water instead of milk and salt instead of sugar. Use to wrap scrambled egg or shredded vegetables.

鹹菜餅 Salted Vegetable Patties

Ingredients:
3 cups plain wheat flour, 1/3 cups shredded lean pork, 3 tablespoons oil, 1/2 cup salted vegetable, 2/3 cup oil
(I) 1 tablespoon soy sauce, 1/3 teaspoon salt, 2/3 tablespoon sugar, 2 teaspoons ginger wine, $1^1/2$ teaspoons cornstarch powder
(II) 1 teaspoon MSG, 1/2 teaspoon pepper, 2 tablespoons cornstarch paste

Method:
1. Blend flour with enough water to make a smooth dough. Divide into pieces of 4-5 ounces each. Shape each into a round 2" in diameter and 1" thick.
2. Marinate the shredded pork with ingredients (I) for 20 minutes. Pour 3 tablespoons of oil into a frying pan. Stir-fry the pork till the color changes. Remove, leaving the juice in the pan. Add the salted vegetable. Stir-fry till it smells good. Add the shredded pork again and stir-fry for a while. Add ingredients (II) to make the dish creamy. Remove.
3. Place $1^1/2$ tablespoons of filling in the center of each round piece. Pinch the edges together carefully. Flatten each one slightly and gently.
4. Pour 2/3 cup of oil into a frying pan. Fry the patties over low heat, turning to cook on both sides. Fry till the surface is scorched and crisp. Serve.

Note:
All fried food should be drained on absorbent paper or it will taste greasy and unpleasant.

豆沙餅 Red Bean Pancakes

Ingredients:
8 ounces red beans, 2/3 cup oil
(I) 1/3 cup shortening or lard, $10^1/2$ ounces brown sugar, 2-3 tablespoons water
(II) $2^3/4$ cups plain wheat flour, 1/2 teaspoon salt, 1-2 tablespoons lard

Method:
1. Pick over the red beans. Soak in water to cover by 2 inches for 4-6 hours.
2. Drain the beans. Bring a pot of water to a boil. Add the beans and cook till they split open. Drain, let cool, and put into a food processor with 1/2 cup of water. Mash. Pour the mashed beans into a clean cheesecloth bag. Tie tightly. Press out the moisture. The mashed red bean is ready when it is no longer wet.
3. Put ingredients (I) in a frying pan. Boil over low heat. When the sugar melts and the mixture becomes shiny and brown, add the mashed red bean. Over a medium flame, stir till half the water evaporates. The red bean paste should be dark red and smell good. Remove and divide into $2^1/2$ ounces balls.
4. Blend ingredients (II) with some water and knead to a smooth dough. Cut into 4-ounce pieces. Shape each piece into a round, flatten, then roll into 1"-thick wrapping skin. Place a red bean ball in the center and pinch the edges together carefully.
5. Fry as in Salted Vegetable Patties.

Notes:
1. If a food processor is not available, put the cooked red beans in a clean cloth bag. Tie tightly. Soak the bag in water. Rub the bag with your hands in the water till the bean skins are crushed and the beans are mashed. Let the bag stand still for a white. Pour off some water when the mash settles. Pack into another bag, then press out the moisture.
2. With crushed skin, the red bean mash is more nutritious but less smooth.

燒賣 Steamed Shao-Mai

Ingredients:
13 ounces very lean ground pork, 24 medium to large shelled shrimps, 24 pieces wonton skin (or dumpling skin)
(I) 1 teaspoon salt, 1 tablespoon ginger wine, 1/2 teaspoon MSG, 1/2 teaspoon pepper
(II) $1^1/2$ teaspoons ginger wine, 2 teaspoons cornstarch

Method:
1. Blend ground pork well with ingredients (I) and let stand for 20 minutes. Rinse the shrimps. Marinate with ingredients (II) for 20 minutes.
2. Place $1^1/2$ tablespoons of filling in the center of each wonton skin. Pinch the edges up to make a flower pattern. Leave a hole in the center to let the filling show a little bit. Place a shrimp in the center.
3. Place shao-mai in a steamer and steam for 25 minutes. Serve.

Note:
If you do not like shrimps, you can use quail eggs instead.

鍋貼
Kuo-Tieh (Fried Dumplings)

Ingredients:

3 cups all-purpose flour (or use ready-made dumpling skins), 10 ounces lean ground pork, 1/3 cup chopped chives, 1/4 cup oil, 1/3 cup water

(I) 2/3 teaspoon salt, 1/3 teaspoon MSG, 1/3 teaspoon pepper, 1 1/2 teaspoons ginger wine, 1 1/2 teaspoons sesame oil

Method:

1. Mix flour with enough water to knead into a smooth dough. Roll into a long roll as wide as your thumb. Cut into 1" pieces. Flatten and lightly flour each piece and roll into a round skin that is thick in the center and thin at the edges.
2. Blend the ground pork and chopped chives with ingredients (I). Put 2 teaspoons of this filling in the center of each wrapper. Pinch the edges up. The bottom of each dumpling should be flat.
3. Pour oil into a frying pan. Heat slightly. Arrange dumplings in the pan and fry over medium heat for 1 minute. Turn the heat to high and add the water. Fry over medium heat with the cover on. When the water is absorbed and there's a sizzling sound, remove the lid. Remove when the bottom of the dumplings is slightly scorched.

Note:

You can add 110°F water to the flour to make the dumpling skin more elastic and soft.

水餃

Shuei-Chiao (Boiled Pork Dumplings)

Ingredients:

10 ounces Chinese cabbage (or leek, chive, turnip, or white Chinese cabbage), 13 ounces lean ground pork, 3 cups all-purpose flour (or 20 ounces ready-made dumpling skins)

(I) 1 teaspoon salt, 1 teaspoon sugar, 1/3 teaspoon MSG, 1/2 teaspoon white pepper, 1 tablespoon ginger wine, 1/2 tablespoon sesame oil, 1/3 cup water or soup stock

Method:

1. Rinse the Chinese cabbage and blanch to soften. Chop and squeeze dry. Add to the ground pork and ingredients (I). Blend well. Remember to add the water slowly while stirring clockwise, to make sure the water is absorbed completely.
2. Knead the flour and some water into a dough. Follow the method used in Fried Dumplings to make dumpling skins. Put 2/3 tablespoon of filling in the center of each skin. Pinch the edges up to make a boatlike shape.
3. Bring 3 cups of water to a boil. Put the dumplings in, one by one. Stir clockwise with a spatula or the dumplings will stick to the bottom. Return to a boil. Add a cup of cold water and cook, covered, till boiling again. Add water again. Repeat twice more, so that the pork filling can be well cooked. After the third boiling, turn off the heat. Remove and serve.

Notes:

1. Turnip, leek, and white Chinese cabbage can be prepared the same as Chinese cabbage, but instead of blanching to soften, you can sprinkle some salt on the chopped vegetable, then squeeze dry.
2. Scalded dough can also be used to make dumpling skins.

燙

麵

類

Scalded Dough

How to make scalded dough

1. Measure flour. Sift, then add lard to it.
2. Heat water to boiling.
3. Add hot water to flour and blend with chopsticks.
4. Blend flour with water roughly.
5. Cover with a piece of wet cloth for about 10 minutes.
6. Knead the flour mixture to make it a dough. It will not look smooth.
7. Add flour or water as needed to make it moderately smooth. Cover with a wet cloth. Let stand for 20 minutes.
8, 9. Knead again carefully. (It is said that the dough will be in its best condition after 300 pushes.)
10. The dough now is ready for making dimsum.
11. If there is any dough left, remember to cover it with a piece of wet cloth, or it will dry out and turn hard.

韭菜盒子
Leek Ho-Tzu (Leek Boxes)

Ingredients:

42 ounces leeks, 1 cup bean threads, 2 soft spiced bean curd, 1/2 cup chopped egg pancake, 3 cups plain wheat flour, some 160°F water, 1/3 cup oil

(I) 2 teaspoons salt, 1/2 teaspoon MSG, 1/2 teaspoon sesame oil

Method:

1. Remove old and withered leaves from leeks. Wash clean. Soak the bean threads in water for 10 minutes. Dice leeks, bean thread, and spiced bean curds. Blend well with chopped egg pancake and ingredients (I).
2. Make scalded dough according to the steps in "How to make scalded dough." Cut the dough into 4-ounce pieces. Use a rolling pin to roll each part into a round 4-6 inches wide. Spread filling on each piece. (The filling should cover around 80% of the piece. Fold it up to make a semicircle. Trim the edge with the brim of a bowl.
3. Put oil in a frying pan. Put ho-tzu in. Fry over low to medium heat for 10-15 minutes turning once. Remove when the surface is browned. Serve.

Note:

Instead of frying, you can bake ho-tzu without oil. They will be chewy but not crispy.

蔥油餅
Scallion Pancakes

Ingredients:

3 cups plain wheat flour, some 140°F water, 1 cup finely chopped scallions, 2 teaspoons salt, 1 cup lard or vegetable oil

Method:

1. Make scalded dough and divide into pieces about 5-6 1/2 ounces each.
2. Roll out each piece 1/8" thick. Brush lard or oil on each piece. Sprinkle chopped scallions and salt on top. Roll it up. Close two ends by pinching them hard. Squeeze it into a ball and roll out again into a round piece.
3. Put a tablespoon of oil in a frying pan. Fry each pancake over medium heat till browned. (Turn during frying.) Remove and serve.

Note:

Pastry made from scalded dough tastes crispier.

家常菜餅

Homemade Vegetable pancakes

Ingredients:

31 ounces white Chinese cabbage, 2 teaspoons salt, 8 ounces ground pork, 1 bean curd, 3 cups plain wheat flour, some 140°-160° F water, 1 cup oil

(I) 1/2 tablespoon soy sauce, 1 tablespoon salt, 1/2 tablespoon sugar, 1/2 teaspoon MSG, 1/2 tablespoon pepper, 1 tablespoon cornstarch, 1/2 tablespoon sesame oil

Method:

1. Wash white Chinese cabbage. Remove old and withered leaves and stems. Rub with the salt till soft. Wash salt off. Squeeze dry. Chop.
2. Blend ground pork, chopped cabbage, mashed bean curd, and ingredients (I) to make filling.
3. Make scalded dough. Knead till the dough is smooth and shining. Divide into 5-ounce pieces. Shape each piece into a bag with your hands. Put 1-2 tablespoons filling in each bag. Close the bag and press each one to make it flat.
4. Put oil in a frying pan. Fry pancakes over low to medium heat till both sides are browned, about 20-25 minutes. Serve.

Note:

The pancakes can also be baked without oil on baking sheet.

碎肉煎餅

Grilled Ground Meat Pancakes

Ingredients:

2 onions, 1 cup oil, 3 cups all-purpose flour, 5 ounces ground pork or beef, some 160°F water (optional)

(I) 2 teaspoons salt, 1/2 teaspoon sugar, 1/2 teaspoon MSG, 1/2 teaspoon pepper

Method:

1. Peel onions and cut into 1/4" threads.
2. Put 3 tablespoons oil in a frying pan. Fry the shredded onion till soft. While still hot, mix with flour, ground meat, and ingredients (I). Hot water can be added if the paste is too thick.
3. Put 3-4 tablespoons oil in a frying pan. Heat slightly. Put 8 tablespoons of paste in the pan. Fry till both sides are browned and crisp. Serve.

Notes:

1. This way of cooking pancakes saves a lot of time spent in preparing dough and filling.
2. Eggplant, pumpkin, gourd, string beans, and other vegetable can be used to replace the onion.

蒸餃
Steamed Dumplings

Ingredients:

13 ounces ground pork, 3 cups plain wheat flour, some 160°F water

(I) 1 tablespoon ginger wine, $1/2$ teaspoon pepper, $1^1/2$ teaspoons salt, $1/2$ teaspoon MSG, 2 teaspoons sesame oil, 3 tablespoons soup stock

Method:

1. Blend ground pork and ingredients (I) well, stirring till it is very sticky.
2. Make scalded dough. Knead to a smooth long roll. Cut into $1/2$-ounce sections. Roll each section into a round that is thick in the center, thin at the edges. Put 1 tablespoon of filling on each skin. Wrap it up.
3. Put a piece of wet cloth on the bottom of a steamer. Put the dumplings on top. Steam over a high flame for 8 minutes. (The water in the steamer should be boiling before you put the dumplings in.) Serve.

Note:

The skin of steamed dumplings is more elastic than the skin of boiled dumplings.

荷葉餅
Doubled Pancakes

Ingredients:

2 cups all-purpose flour, $1^1/4$ cups cake flour, some 160 F water, 2 tablespoons lard

Method:

1. Sift the flour and mix together well. Make scalded dough and divide into 2-ounce balls. Flatten each one.
2. Brush some lard on one side of each piece. Overlap two pieces, oiled side in. Roll into a pancake with a rolling pin. It is very important that you do not let the edges curl up.
3. Bake each pancake in a clean frying pan over low to medium heat. (Do not put any oil in the pan.) Bake till the color changes, turn, and bake for $1/2$ minute more. Remove.
4. Tear the pancake into two thin and soft pieces. Use to wrap some filling or Peking duck slices, sweet sauce, and scallion.

發 麵 類

Leavened Dough

How to make leavened dough

1. (A) Baking Powder
      It is used to make cakes and biscuits. The amount used depends on the pastry you want to make.
   (B) Yeast Cake
      It is used to make man-tou (steamed bread), yiu-tiao (twisted cruller), and rolls or buns. $1^1/2$-2 teaspoons can leaven 6 to 10 cups of flour. Keep refrigerated.
   (C) Yeast Powder (in glass bowl)
      This is the same as yeast cake in function.
   (D) Two different stages of leavening are shown in the glass and the bowl.
2. Prepare some warm water.
3. Put 1 teaspoon of sugar in the warm water.
4. Stir it well.
5. Put 1 teaspoon of yeast powder in the solvent.
6. Do not stir. Let stand for 7-10 minutes. When there are bubbles on the surface, the solvent is ready.
7. Mix the solvent with sifted flour. Add some warm water, if necessary.
8. Knead to a dough. Put in a basin.
9. Use your fingers to make some holes in the dough. Sprinkle with water.
10. Cover with a piece of wet cloth. Let stand for 3 hours at normal indoor temperature. The cooler the day is, the longer it will take for the dough to be completely leavened.
11. Two hours later.
12. When it is completely leavened, knead till smooth and shiny. The leavened dough is ready now. If you let it stand for another 20 minutes, the dough will be even better for making pastry.

小籠包　Steamed Small Pork Buns

Ingredients:
some warm water, 1/2 teaspoon sugar, 1 teaspoon yeast powder, 2 cups plain wheat flour, 1 tablespoon lard
(I) 20 ounces lean ground pork, 1 1/2 teaspoons salt, 1 tablespoon ginger wine, 1/3 teaspoon pepper, 1/2 tablespoon sesame oil, 4 tablespoons water, 1/2 teaspoon MSG
(II) 1/3 cup tender ginger shreds, 3 tablespoons soy sauce, 3 tablespoons vinegar

Method:
1. Make leavened dough.
2. Divide into small pieces, about 1 1/3 ounces each.
3. Mix ingredients (I) well to make filling.
4. Roll out each piece of dough to a round that is thick in the center, thin at the edges. Wrap 1 tablespoon of filling in each skin to make a bun.
5. Let stand for 3-5 minutes. Steam for 10 minutes. Serve.

湯包　Steamed Juicy Pork Buns

Ingredients:
Ingredients for filling are the same as for Steamed Small Pork Buns.
some warm water, 1/2 teaspoon sugar, 1 teaspoon yeast powder, 2 cups plain wheat flour, 1 tablespoon lard
(I) 20 ounces lean ground pork, 1 1/2 teaspoons salt, 1 tablespoon ginger wine, 1/3 teaspoon pepper, 1/2 tablespoon sesame oil, 4 tablespoons water, 1/2 teaspoon MSG
(II) 10 ounces pig's skin, 10 ounces chicken feet, some water, 1 scallion, 1 ginger root

Method:
1. Dice the pig's skin. Boil with all other ingredients in (II). Let simmer till there are 1 1/2 cups of liquid left. Strain. Let the liquid stand till it becomes jellied. Dice it. Mix with ingredients (I) to make filling.
2. Make small pork buns according to the method used in Steamed Small Pork Buns. The difference between the two is that the filling of the juicy buns is very juicy.
3. Small juicy buns can be served in soup. You can use clear broth, or make soup by mixing a tablespoon of soy sauce with boiling water, some egg pancake shreds, and preserved vegetable shreds or ginger shreds and minced parsley.

菜肉大包　Steamed Pork and Vegetable Buns

Ingredients:
some warm water, 1 tablespoon sugar, 1 1/2 teaspoons yeast powder, 3 cups plain wheat flour, 20 ounces white Chinese cabbage, salted vegetable, or cabbage, 13 ounces lean ground pork
(I) 1 teaspoon salt, 1/3 tablespoon soy sauce, 1/2 teaspoon MSG, 1/2 tablespoon ginger wine, 1/2 teaspoon pepper, 1/2 tablespoon sesame oil

Method:
1. Make leavened dough. Divide into small pieces, 2 1/4-4 ounces each.
2. Wash the cabbage and chop. Blend with ground pork and ingredients (I).
3. Roll the dough into round pieces that are thick in the center. thin on the edges. Put 2 tablespoons of filling in the middle. Hold in one hand. Press the filling with your thumb. Fold the edges up with the other hand.
4. Cover all buns with a piece of wet cloth. Let stand for 20 minutes. Put a piece of wet cloth on the bottom of a steamer. Put the buns on top. Steam over a high flame for 25 minutes.

Note:
Steamed buns taste best when they are still hot.

花捲

Hua-Chuan (Steamed Twist)

Ingredients:

some warm water, 1¹/₂ tablespoons sugar, 2 teaspoons yeast powder, 3 cups all-purpose flour, 3/4 cup cake flour, 1¹/₂ teaspoons vinegar, 2 tablespoons lard

(I) 2 tablespoons lard, some chopped scallion; ¹/₂ tablespoon salt

Method:

1. Make leavened dough.
2. Roll the dough out to a large, thin piece with a rolling pin. Spread ingredients (I) evenly on top. Roll it up from two opposite sides.
3. Cut the roll into several sections. Fold each section up from two ends to make a square.
4. Press with a chopstick in the middle. Cover with a wet cloth for 20 minutes. Steam for 20-30 minutes. Serve.

Note:

1. Hua-chuan should be served while still hot.
2. You can twist the dough in your own way.

饅頭

Man-Tou (Steamed Bread)

Ingredients:

some warm water, 1¹/₂ tablespoons sugar, 2 teaspoons yeast powder, 3 cups all-purpose flour, 3/4 cup cake flour, 1¹/₂ teaspoons vinegar, 2 tablespoons lard

Method:

1. Knead flour to a leavened dough.
2. Knead to a long roll, 3" in diameter. Cut into 2" sections. Let stand for 20 minutes. Steam over a high flame for 20-30 minutes. Serve.

Notes:

1. It is said that man-tou tastes best after 300 pushes during kneading.
2. Sliced cold man-tou can be served as bread.

銀絲捲

Ying-Su-Chuan (Steamed Shredded Rolls)

Ingredients:

some warm water, 1¹/₂ tablespoons sugar, 2¹/₂ teaspoons yeast powder, 3/4 cup all-purpose flour, 3 cups cake flour, 1¹/₂ teaspoons vinegar, 2 tablespoons lard
(I) ¹/₂ cup lard, ¹/₂ cup sugar

Method:

1. Make leavened dough.
2. Roll the dough into a piece 1/8" thick. Spread ingredients (I) evenly on top. Fold into a strip 2¹/₄" wide.
3. Coat a knife blade with oil. Shred the strip. Divide all the shreds into 5 bundles. Pull each bundle gently.
4. Wind each bundle around a chopstick. Remove the chopstick. Cover all the shredded rolls with a wet cloth. Steam over a high flame for 20 minutes. Serve.

Notes:

1. You can use a third of the dough to make skin to wrap the shredded dough. The shredded rolls will look like man-tou this way.
2. Steamed shredded rolls can also be deep-fried, then served.
3. Minced ham can be added to ingredients (I).

千層糕

Layer Cake

Ingredients:

5 ounces pork fat, 1/3 cup sugar, 2 tablespoons rendered lard, 4 tablespoons green and red papaya shreds, 2-3 tablespoons raisins
(I) 3 cups cake flour, some warm water, 1¹/₂ teaspoons yeast powder, 1 teaspoon sugar

Method:

1. Make leavened dough.
2. Chop the pork fat. Marinate with sugar and let stand overnight.
3. Roll the dough out to a thin piece. Brush on some oil. Spread a thin layer of chopped pork fat, papaya shreds, and raisins evenly in the middle. They should cover about one third of the piece.
4. Fold one third up. Brush on some oil. Spread some chopped fat, papaya shreds, and raisins on top. Fold the other third up.
5. Repeat step 4 to make a square cake with layers. Garnish with papaya shreds and raisins.
6. Cover with a wet cloth for 20 minutes. Steamed over a high flame for 20 minutes. Remove and serve.

Notes:

1. Minced ham can be used to replace the papaya shreds and raisins if you do not like sweet food. Remember to use less sugar when marinating the pork fat.
2. You can divide the dough into 4-5 parts and dye them different colors. Put them together to make a colorful layer cake.

45

破酥包
Po-Su Buns

Ingredients:
10 ounces leavened dough, 10 ounces scalded dough, 7 ounces oiled dough

(I) 2 chicken breasts(boned and minced), 10 ounces lean ground pork, 6 tablespoons chopped bamboo shoot

(II) 2 teaspoons salt, 2 teaspoons sesame oil, $1/2$ tablespoon cornstarch, $1/2$ tablespoon ginger wine, $1^1/2$ teaspoons sugar, $1/2$ teaspoon MSG, 2 tablespoons water

Method:
1. Knead leavened dough and scalded dough together. Let stand for 30 minutes. Roll out to a large piece. Roll oiled dough into a large piece on top. Roll up to make a long stick. Cut into pieces about 4-5 ounces each.
2. Mix ingredients (I) and (II) to make filling.
3. Roll each piece of dough into a round skin that is thick in the center, thin at the edges. Wrap 2 tablespoons of filling in each skin to make a bun.
4. Cover the buns with a wet cloth for 20 minutes. Steam over a high flame for 20 minutes. Serve.

Note:
Red bean mash can also be used as filling if you like sweet food.

簡易小麵包
Easy-to-Make Rolls

Ingredients:
2 teaspoons yeast powder, $1/2$ cup warm milk, 2 cups all-purpose flour, 1 egg

(I) 1 teaspoon sugar, 1/3 cup warm water
(II) 1 teaspoon slat, $1^1/2$ tablespoons melted butter
(III) 3 egg yolks, 1 egg white

Method:
1. Blend yeast powder well with ingredients (I). Let stand till bubbles appear on the surface.
2. Put ingredients (II)and warm milk in a small saucepan. Stir gently. Add ingredients (III). Beat well with an eggbeater.
3. Sift the flour twice. Divide into 3 parts. Add them to the egg batter gradually. Knead to a dough. Do not add any flour during kneading. Knead till the dough is shing smooth.
4. Put the dough in a plastic bag. Squeeze the air out of the bag and tie it tightly. Wrap in a cloth bag. Refrigerate for 10 hours. (The temperature in the refrigerator should be aorund 40°F.)
5. Divide the dough into pieces about 4 ounces each. Put each piece in a small mold or muffin cup. (Before you do this, coat each mold with butter, refrigerate for 10 minutes, and flour lightly.) Cover each one with a piece of cellophane or wax paper. Let stand for 30-40 minutes.
6. Remove cellophane. Sprinkle water on each roll. Put in a preheated 420°F oven and bake for 15-20 minutes.
7. Beat the egg well. Brush some egg on each roll. Put the rolls back in the oven for a while. Remove. The rolls look shiny and taste delicious.

水蒸蛋糕

Steamed cake

Ingredients:

2 cups cake flour, 2 teaspoons baking powder, 4 eggs, 7 ounces sugar, $1^{1}/_{2}$ teaspoons wine, 2 tablespoons raisins

Method:

1. Mix flour and baking powder well. Sift twice.
2. Beat eggs and sugar well. Beat till some bubbles stay on the beater for a while when you remove the beater.
3. Add wine, flour, and part of the raisins. Mix well.
4. Spread cellophane on the bottom of an 8" mold. Brush some oil on the cellophane. Pour in the batter. Steam over a high flame for 20-25 minutes. (The water in the steamer should be boiling before you put in the mold.)
5. After 15 minutes of steaming, spread the remaining raisins on the cake. Cover the steamer and continue to steam till done.

Notes:

1. If you put in all the raisins at once, they will all sink to the bottom of the cake.
2. Do not over- or under-beat the eggs.

馬來糕

Sponge Cake, Cantonese Style

Ingredients:

10 eggs, 13 ounces oil

(I) 1 cup all-purpose flour, 1 cup cake flour, $^{1}/_{2}$ cup cornstarch, 20 ounces sugar

(II) 3-6 vanilla beans, $1^{1}/_{3}$ cups milk, 1/3 teaspoon salt

(III) 1 ounce baking powder, $^{1}/_{4}$ cup water

Method:

1. Mix ingredients (I) well. Sift.
2. Beat eggs well. Strain.
3. Blend ingredients (II) well.
4. Add the flour mixture to beaten eggs. Mix well. Add ingredients (II). Still stirring, add the baking powder dissolved in water. Mix well.
5. Spread cellophane in an 8" mold. Brush oil on the cellophane. Pour in the mixture. Steam over a high flame for 25 minutes. Serve.

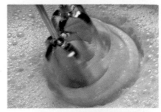

Note:

A carton or hard paper box can be used if a mold is not available.

開口笑

Smiling Muffins

Ingredients:

2 eggs, 1¹/₂ tablespoons lard, 2/3 cup sugar, some water, 1/3 cup sesame seeds, 1 pan of oil for frying

(I) 3 cups cake flour, 1 cup plain wheat flour, 1 teaspoon baking soda, ¹/₂ tablespoon baking powder

Method:

1. Mix ingredients (I) well. Sift.
2. Beat eggs well and add with lard and sugar to ingredients (I). Add enough water to make dough. Cover with a wet cloth for 20 minutes. Shape into a long roll. Cut into several pieces.
3. Rub each piece into a ball. Roll each ball in sesame seeds to coat.
4. Heat oil for frying to over-medium-hot. Fry the balls over a low to medium flame. Keep stirring during frying. Fry till the balls split open and are golden brown. Ladle out. Drain off oil. The muffins taste crispy and delicious.

巧果

Chiao-Kuo (Crunchy Fries)

Ingredients:

2 cups plain wheat flour, 2 tablespoons sugar, ¹/₂ teaspoon salt, 1¹/₂ tablespoons black sesame seeds, 2 tablespoons lard, some water, 1 pan of oil for frying

Method:

1. Knead flour, seasoning, sesame, lard, and water into dough. Let stand for 20 minutes. Roll into a thin piece. Cut into 2"-long strips, then into rhombuses.
2. Slice each piece in the middle. Turn one end over through the cut to make a braid-like pattern. You can also overlap two pieces to make the pattern. Flour lightly.
3. Heat oil to over-medium-hot. Fry over a medium flame till browned. Ladle out, drain, and serve.

火燒

Huo-Shao

Ingredients:
2 cups plain wheat flour, 2 cups cake flour, some water

Method:
1. Mix the flours, add water, and knead to make a dough. Let stand for 25 minutes. Knead again to make it smooth and a little stiff. Divide into 5 or 6 parts.
2. Shape each round, then flatten slightly. Press the edges between thumb and index finger to make a swirl pattern.
3. Place huo-shao in a preheated 450°F oven. Bake till both sides are browned and the center juts out. During baking, remember to turn them over.

Notes:
1. The crust of huo-shao is very hard and crisp. Those who do not have strong teeth can soak it in soup, then eat it.
2. It is one of the most popular Chinese dry provisions.

油煎包

Grilled Pork and Vegetable Buns

Ingredients:
Ingredients for wrapping are the same for Steamed Pork and Vegetable Buns. Ingredients for filling are the same as for Steamed Small Pork Buns. 1 tablespoon sesame seeds, 4 tablespoons oil, 1/2 cup water.

Method:
1. Make leavened dough.
2. Cut into small pieces, each 2 1/2-4 ounces. Make buns according to the steps in Steamed Pork and Vegetable Buns. Toast sesame seeds in a frying pan till they smell good. Put some sesame seeds on top of each bun.
3. Put 3 tablespoons of oil in a large frying pan. Heat for a while. Put in the buns. Cook over a medium flame for 2 minutes. Add some water. Cover and cook for 5-8 minutes. Remember to shake the pan once in a while so the buns can cook evenly.
4. Remove the cover. Put in the remaining oil. Pinch the buns. If they feel elastic, remove. Or you can add 1-2 tablespoons of water, cover the pan, and cook till done.

Note:
Both black and white sesame seeds can be used.

油酥類

Oiled Dough

How to make oiled dough

Oiled dough can be divided into two categories: (A) oiled dough and (B) watered and oiled dough.

A. How to make oiled dough

(The ratio of oil to flour is 1:3.)
1. Mix 3/4 cup of all-purpose flour with 1 1/2 cups of cake flour. Sift.
2. Add 4 ounces of lard. Blend well.

3. Add enough water to make the flour into small lumps. There should be no flour left in the bowl.
4. The picture shows that there is not enough water. Add more.
5. Knead into a smooth and shiny dough. (Because oil and water are hard to mix, the making of oiled dough is very time-consuming.) Let stand for 20 minutes. Knead again. The dough is ready.

How to make pastry with oiled dough

1. Wrapping made from oiled dough is easy to close and easy to shape to various patterns.
2. If you make patterns by cutting, they will look very pretty after baking. Just do not cut so deep that the filling shows.
3. Brush some egg batter on the pastry. After baking, it will look shiny. If you put some soy sauce in the egg batter, the pastry will be dark brown.

B. How to make watered and oiled dough

Watered and oiled dough can be called sandwich dough. It is made by combining oiled filling and watered and oiled wrapping.

(1) Oiled Filling (The ratio of oil to flour is 1:2.)

a. Oiled Dough Filling
1. Mix 1/2 cup of all-purpoise flour with 1 1/4 cups of cake flour. Sift. Add 5-6 ounces lard. 1 tablespoon of sugar can be added.
2. Blend well. Knead. If sugar is used, knead till it melts.
3. Knead dough well. Let stand for 20 minutes. Knead again. It is ready now.

b. Oiled Paste filling
1. Mix 1 to 2 cups of plain wheat flour with equal amount of lard or peanut oil.
2. Fry this mixture in a frying pan till it is a little scorched. Add 1 tablespoon of mixed pepper and salt and 1 tablespoon of ground cinnamon.
3. This fried oiled paste filling is used to make shao-ping (baked cakes) and other special cakes.

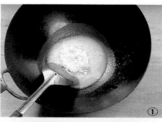

(2) Watered and Oiled Wrapping (The ratio of oil to flour is 1:5.)
1. Mix 1 cup of all-purpose flour, 1 cup of cake flour, and 5 ounces of water. Stir in water gradually.
2. Add 1 ounce of lard. Blend well. Sugar can be added.
3. Knead throughly. Let stand for 20 minutes. Knead again. It is ready now.

Notes:

1. The purposes of adding sugar are:
   a. It will be easier for the pastry to look browned.
   b. The crust will be very crispy. But if you make patterns by cutting, the pastry won't look as good when there is sugar added to the wrapping.
2. Artificial color can be added to the wrapping. For example, 2 tablespoons of curry powder can be used to replace 1 tablespoon of flour when making a curried crust.

How to make pastry with watered and oiled dough

(1)

1. Roll watered and oiled wrapping into a round, thin piece with a rolling pin. Wrap oiled filling up. Pinch edges tightly. Roll out to a large thin, square piece.
2. Fold one third of the piece up. Fold the other one third up to make a rectangle. Roll it slightly to make it larger and thinner. Fold it up as before. Roll out to a 1/4"-thick piece.
3. Roll the piece up to make a long stick. (Its diameter shoudl be less than 1 1/2".) Cut into 1" sections. It is ready to be made into pastry.

(2)

1. Knead oiled filling and watered and oiled wrapping respectively into long rolls. Cut into small sections. (Picture 1 and 2)
2. Press a section of watered and oiled wrapping flat. Roll a section of oiled filling into a ball. Wrap the ball with the wrapping. Roll into a ball. (Picture 3-8)
3. Press each ball slightly. Roll into an oval piece. Roll it up. Repeat the procedure once. It is now ready to be used.
4. Roll out to a thin wrapping to make chrysanthemum pastry, moon cake, Soochow style, bergamot pastry, or pork pastry. (Picture 9-14)
5. The wrapping can be cut to make eyebrow pastry, wheel pastry, shell pastry, or layer pastry. (Pictgure 20-24)
6. Roll out to a long, flat piece to make orchid pastry or flying wheel pastry. (Picture 25, 26)
7. Put pastry in oil heated to 140°-160°F. Fry over a low flame for about 20 minutes. Remove carefully. Drain on paper towels. Serve. (Picture 27)

Notes:

1. Three different oiled doughs. (In Picture 28, starting from the right, oiled dough, oiled filling, and wa-

tered and iled wrapping.)

2. Picture 18 and 19 show paterns made by two pieces of dough in a spiral. You can also create your own patterns.

How to bake pastry at home

1. If an oven is not available, an all-purpose pan can be used instead. Set both the bottom pan and the upper cover over a medium flame. Heat till water sprinkled on them disappears immediately.
2. Brush a thin layer of oil on a baking pan. Put the pastry in the pan. Put a grill in the upper cover. Put the baking pan on. Cover it with the bottom pan. Bake over a low to medium flame for 20 minutes. Remove the cover. The pastry can be turned over if you did not brush egg batter on it. Cover again. Bake over a medium to high flame for 15-20 minutes. Remove and serve.

3. If an oven is available, bake according to the features of each oven.

Notes:
1. When the cover is removed, remember to place it over the flame to keep it hot.
2. The degree of heat used is adjustable according to the amount of oil in the pastry. When the pastry is very oily, use a high flame. When the pastry is not too oily, use a low to medium flame.

 Curry Dumplings

Ingredients: (for 15 dumplings)
13 ounces very lean ground pork or ground beef, 2 tablespoons oil, 2 teaspoons chopped red scallion head
(I) 1¹/₂ tablespoon curry powder, ¹/₂ tablespoon ginger wine, ¹/₂ teaspoon white pepper, ¹/₂ tablespoon cornstarch, 1 teaspoon salt, ¹/₂ teaspoon MSG, 1 teaspoon sugar
Method:
1. Mix ground meat with ingredients (I).
2. Put oil in a frying pan. Fry chopped red scallion head for a while. Add the misture. Quickly stir-fry till pasty.
3. Either oiled dough or watered and oiled dough can be used as wrapping. If you choose the former, do not fry the dumplings. Baking should be the only way. See p.57, picture 22 for details.

 Snowy Coconut Pastry

Ingredients: (for 10 pieces)
1/3 cup cake flour, 1 cup shredded coconut, 6-8 tablespoons sugar, 3-4 tablespoons butter, some condensed milk
Method:
1. Fry the flour over a low to medium flame till lightly browned, or steam for 2-3 minutes. Remove and let dry.
2. Knead coconut, sugar, flour, and butter to a dough. Add condensed milk while kneading. Knead to a moderately soft dough.
3. Divide into small balls and use them as filling. Wrap each one with watered and oiled wrapping. Remember to make cut in each skin, as the filling will swell.
Notes:
Steamed flour makes whiter pastry than fried flour.
See p.57, picture 20 for the wrapping method.

鮮 肉 酥 **Pork Pastry**

Ingredients:
2 tablespoons oil, 10 ounces very lean ground pork, 4 tablespoons chopped salted vegetable root, ¹/₂ tablespoon ginger wine, ¹/₂ teaspoon salt, ¹/₂ teaspoons MSG, ¹/₂ teaspoon white pepper, 2/3 tablespoon cronstarch, ¹/₂ tablespoon sesame oil
Method:
1. Put oil in a frying pan. Stir-fry till all ingredients are well mixed.
2. Wrap filling according the steps shown in the pictures.
Notes:
1. The ingredients for Moon Cake, Soochow Style are the same as for Pork Pastry, but use 2¹/₂ ounces more ground pork.
2. The filling can also be made without frying. Just blend the ingredients well. Remember to put in twice as much cornstarch.
3. The filling can be sweet or salty. You can create you own. See p.57, pictures 14, 15, and 22 for details.

千 層 酥 **Layer Pastry**

Method:
Use red bean mash as filling. See Red Bean Pancakes for the method of preparing red bean mash.
See p.57, pictures 19 and 27 for details.

蘇州月餅

Moon Cakes, Soochow Style

Ingredients: (for 15 pieces)
2 tablespoons oil, 13 ounces very lean ground pork, 4 tablespoons chopped salted vegetable root, 1/2 tablespoon ginger wine, 2/3 tablespoon cornstarch, 1/2 teaspoon salt, 1/2 teaspoon MSG, 1/2 teaspoon white pepper, 1/2 tablespoon sesame oil
Method:
Put oil in a frying pan and stir-fry all ingredients till well mixed. This is the filling.
Note:
You can also blend together all ingredients except oil and use as filling without stir-frying. Remember to use twice as much cornstarch.

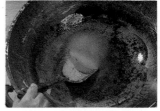

豆沙酥

Red Bean Mash Pastry

Ingredients:
See Red Bean Pancakes for the method of preparing red bean mash. Both oiled dough and watered and oiled dough can be used for wrapping.
Method:
1. Divide red bean mash into balls about 3/4-1 1/3 ounces each.
2. Divide dough into 2-ounce balls.
3. Refer to pictures 1 to 15 on pp.56 and 57 for the method of making the wrappers. Wrap up each red bean mash ball. Bake at 450°F for 30 minutes. See p.57 for details.

一口酥

E-Kuo Pastry

For ingredients, see Pork Pastry.
See the pictures on the right for the method of wrapping.

菊花酥

Chrysanthemum Pastry

Ingredients:

See Red Bean Pancakes for the method of preparing red bean mash. Use it as filling.

Method:

1. See pictures 1 to 15 on pp.56 and 57 for the method of making wrapping.
2. Enclose red bean mash in wrappers. Cut a pattern with a knife. (Picture 1 on the right)
3. Picture 2 on the right shows the cut pastry.
4. Fry over a low flame till done. See picture 28 on p.57.

車輪酥

Wheel Pastry

Use red bean mash as filling.

How to make red bean mash:

1. Wash red beans clean. Soak in water for 4 hours or overnight. (Picture 1)
2. Bring a saucepan of water to a boil. Add the red beans. Simmer till they are paste-like. See picture 2 on p.61.
3. Put the cooked red beans in a food processor or blender and mash. (Picture 2) Squeeze out the water.
4. Fry dry red bean mash with lard till it smells good. Add sugar. Fry till the mash no longer sticks to the pan and the spatula. See picture 3 and 4 on the right and picture 3 on p.61.

夾肉小燒餅

Shao-Ping Sandwiches

Ingredients: (for 15 pieces)
2 cups all-purpose flour, 1¹/₂ cups cake flour, 2/3 cup oiled paste filling, 1/3 cup white sesame seeds, 7-8 ounces spiced beef shank or spiced pork meat

Method:
1. Mix the flours together. Add 3 tablespoons of oiled paste filling and enough water to make a dough. Let stand for 20 minutes. Knead again till smooth and shiny.
2. Roll out to a large, thin piece with a rolling pin. Spread half of the remaining oiled paste filling on top. Roll it up to make a long stick. Roll the stick up to make a small pack. Roll out to a large thin piece again. Spread the remaining oiled paste filling on top. Roll it up to make a long stick. Cut it into small pieces about 2¹/₂ ounces each.
3. Roll each small piece into a round. Brush with water. Spread some sesame seeds on each piece. Press hard on the side without sesame seeds.
4. Heat an all-purpose pan and brush with oil. Put shao-ping in, sesame side down. Cover the pan. Bake over a medium flame for 10 minutes. Remove the cover and turn, sesame side up. Bake for another 10-15 minutes. Serve. Cut each shao-ping open from the side and stuff with sliced meat.

See pictures B₁-B₃ on p.55.

燒餅

Shao-Ping (Baked Cakes)

Ingredients: (for 15 pieces)
2 cups all-purpose flour, 1¹/₂ cups cake flour, ¹/₂ cup oiled paste filling, ¹/₃ cup white sesame seeds

Method:
1. Mix the flours together. Add 2 tablespoons of oiled paste filling and enough water to make a dough. Let stand for 20 minutes. Knead again till smooth and shiny.
2. Rub into a 1¹/₂"-diameter long roll. Cut into small pieces about 3¹/₂-4 ounces each.
3. Roll each one into a thin oval. Spread ¹/₂ tablespoon of oiled paste filling on top. Roll it up. Press one fourth of it near one end flat, then roll the remaining part to 2¹/₈"-wide piece. Roll it up to make a square roll.
3. Brush some water on each shao-ping. Spread sesame seeds on top. Roll with a rolling pin into a 6"-long, 2³/₄"-wide oval piece. Keep sesame side down. Put in a frying pan. Cover the pan. Bake over a low to medium flame for 15 minutes, turning at least once.

米飯類

Rice

How to prepare bamboo leaves

1. You can find the following kinds of bamboo leaves on the market.
   a. large bamboo leaves, dry or fresh
   b. brown, spotted bamboo leaves (Lotus leaves can be used together with bamboo leaves. Banana leaves and vegetable leaves can also be used.)

Picture 1
Whether leaves are dry or fresh, boil them in water to soften them.
Picture 2
Wipe both sides clean.
Picture 3 and 4
Trim the leaves by cutting off the points and stems.
Picture 5
Put two leaves together back to back. Use them to make tsung-tzu.

湖州肉粽

Tsung-Tzu (Glutinous Rice Dumplings), Hu-Chow Style

Ingredients:

10 ounces pork belly, 20 ounces round glutinous rice, 1/3 teaspoon salt, bamboo leaves, straw

(I) 1/3 cup soy sauce, rice wine, MSG

Method:

1. Remove skin from the pork belly. Cut into 2"-wide strips. Soak with ingredients (I) overnight.
2. Wash the rice. Blend well with salt and the sauce used to soak the meat. Let stand for 10 minutes. Blend again.
3. Put 2 pieces of bamboo leaves together back to back. Fold one fourth of the leaves from the stems up to make a right angle. Put 2 tablespoons of rice in. Lay meat strips on top. Put another 2 tablespoons of rice on top of the meat. (Remember to press the rice hard.)

4. Cover the rice by folding over the remaining part of the leaves. Fold the ends at an angle. Wrap neatly and tightly.
5. Fasten tightly with straw.
6. Put tsung-tzu in a large saucepan. Add cold water to cover by 3". Bring to a boil over a high flame. Simmer over a low to medium flame for 4 hours. Turn off the heat and let stand, covered, for 1 hour. Remove and serve.

湖州豆沙粽

Red Bean Mash Tsung-Tzu, Hu-Chow Style

Ingredients:

8 ounces pork fat, 21 ounces sugar, 10 ounces red beans, 20 ounces round glutinous rice, bamboo leaves

Method:

1. Cut pork fat into 2"-long, 1/2"-wide strips. Marinate with 2/3 cup of sugar overnight.
2. Refer to Red Bean Pancakes for the method of preparing red bean mash.
3. Wrap each pork fat strip with 2 tablespoons of red bean mash. Form into an oval.
4. Make tsung-tzu according to the steps in Pork Tsung-Tzu, Hu-Chow Style.

Notes:

1. Tsung-Tzu will taste even better if you boil pork tsung-tsu and red bean mash tsung-tzu together.
2. If one bamboo leaf is not long enough, you can use another one together with the short one.

碱粽
Chien Tsung

Ingredients:

21 ounces round glutinous rice, 0.4 ounce sodium carbonate powder, bamboo leaves, straw, 1/2 teaspoon borax

Method:

1. Wash the rice. Blend with sodium carbonate powder. Let stand for 1-2 hours.
2. Use only 1 leaf to make each chien-tsung. Do not put too much rice in tsung-tzu.
3. Put tsung-tzu in a saucepan full of water. Add borax. Bring to a boil. Let boil for 4 hours. Turn off the heat. Let stand, covered, for 1 hour. Serve.

Notes:

1. Tsung-tzu will look transparent if you add the borax to the water.
2. If you use the brown, spotted bamboo leaves, do not add borax during boiling.
3. To eat chien-tsung, you can dip it in syrup or in a mixture of soy sauce and pepper.

螺角粽
Spiral Tsung-Tzu

Ingredients:

21 ounces glutinous rice, 1/2 teaspoon salt, 6 1/2 ounces red beans (or green beans, peanuts, or black dates), 20 fresh bamboo leaves, 1 bundle of straw

Method:

1. Wash the rice. Drain. Blend with salt. Wash the red beans. If you use peanuts or black dates, soak in water for 2-4 hours.
2. Blend the rice and red beans together. Put 2 leaves together back to back. Fold leaf points up to make a sugar-cone shape. Put rice in the cone, stuffing it in hard. Do not leave any space bfetween the grains of rice.
3. Fold the remaining part to make a triangular shape. Tie it with straw.
4. Bring to a boil according to the steps in Tsung-Tzu, Hu-Chow Style.

Notes:

1. If you use rice only, the tsung-tzu is called crystal tsung-tzu. To eat, dip in sugar or a sauce.
2. There's another way to eat this tsung-tzu. Let it get cold, remove the leaves and flour it. Fry in over-medium-hot oil till golden brown. Tsung-tzu tastes very good after frying.

粿粽

Kuo Tsung

Ingredients:

6 cups boiling water, 1/2 cup dried turnip shreds, 8 ounces pork belly, 4 tablespoons dried baby shrimps, 4 tablespoons oil, 4 tablespoons minced red scallion head, bamboo leaves, straw

(I) 21 ounces tsai-lai rice powder and 3 ounces glutinous rice powder

(II) 1 teaspoon salt, 1 1/2 tablespoons soy sauce, 1/2 tablespoon sugar, 1/3 teaspoon MSG, 1 tablespoon cornstarch paste, 1/2 tablespoon wine

Method:

1. Mix ingredients (I) well. Stir in boiling water, little by little.
2. Soak dried turnip shreds in water for 10 minutes. Squeeze dry. Cut pork into large cubes. Soak dried baby shrimps in water for 20 minutes. Mix together ingredients (II).
3. Put oil in a frying pan. Stir-fry minced red scallion head for a few seconds. Add dried baby shrimps, pork cubes, and dried turnip shreds. Add ingredients (II) during stir-frying. Stir-fry for 3 minutes. Remove. This is the filling.
4. Brush oil evenly on the inner side of bamboo leaves. Fold it up. Put 1 1/2 tablespoons of the rice powder paste in the bottom. Put 1 tablespoon of filling on top. Cover with 1 1/2 tablespoons of rice powder paste. Wrap it up to make tsung-tzu. Put in a steamer. Steam for 40 minutes. Remember to remove the cover once every 10 minutes, or tsung-tzu will split open.

Notes:

1. Mustard head, pumpkin, spinach, carrot, etc., can all be used as ingredients.
2. You can also use 21 ounces glutinous rice and 2 ounces of flour to replace the rice powder.

河粉捲

Ho-Fen Rolls (Rice Rolls)

Ingredients:

10 ounces fresh shelled shrimps, 1 tablespoon chopped pork fat, 2 tablespoons oil, 21 ounces ho-fen, 1/2 tablespoon lard, 2 tablespoons chopped parsley

(I) 1 tablespoon ginger wine, 1/3 teaspoon salt, 1/3 teaspoon pepper, 1/3 tablespoon cornstarch

(II) 2 tablespoons seafood sauce, 1 teaspoon salt, 1/3 teaspoon MSG, 1/2 tablespoon cornstarch, 1/2 cup soup stock, 2 tablespoons chopped parsley

Method:

1. Wash the shrimps. Marinate with ingredients (I) and chopped pork fat for 20 minutes.
2. Stir-fry ingredients (II) with oil. Remove when it comes to a boil.
3. Open ho-fen out to a large piece. Cut in two. Spread shrimps and pork fat mixture evenly on top. Roll it up to make two 1 1/2"-wide sticks.
4. Brush lard on a plate. Put ho-fen rolls on top. Steam for 7-8 minutes over a medium to high flame. (Put ho-fen rolls in the steamer after the water in the bottom is boiling.) Pour ingredients (II) on top. Serve.

Note:

Pork and beef can be used to replace shrimps.

河粉湯
Ho-Fen Soup

Ingredients:

10 ounces shredded beef, 10 ounces white Chinese cabbage, 4 tablespoons oil, 1 table-spoon minced scallion, 8 cups soup stock, 26 ounces ho-fen

(I) 1/2 tablespoon ginger wine, 1/2 teaspoon salt, 1/3 teaspoon five-spice powder, 1 teaspoon sesame oil, 1 tablespoon cornstarch, 5 tablespoons water

(II) 1 1/2 teaspoons salt, 1/2 teaspoon MSG, 1/2 tablespoon soy sauce

Method:

1. Marinate shredded beef with ingredients (I) for 20 minutes. Wash white Chinese cabbage. Cut into long strips. Cut ho-fen into 3/8"-wide strips.

2. Put oil in a frying pan. Stir-fry the minced scallion for a few seconds. Add the beef. Stir-fry till its color changes. Pour in the soup stock. Add ho-fen and ingredients (II). Bring to a boil. Add the Chinese cabbage. Let boil for 2 minutes. Remove and serve.

Notes:

1. Ho-fen can be cooked by boiling, stir-frying, steaming, and deep-frying.

2. Chicken or pork can be used instead of beef.

壽司二式

Sushi, Two Different Styles

Ingredients:

3 cups cooked rice, 4-6 pieces laver, 20 flat fried bean curds, 2 eggs, (Cook it to make eggpancake first, then cut it into shreds.) 1 large piece of pickled ginger (shredded), shredded cucumber, pork fluff, 1 tablespoon sesame seeds

(I) 3 tablespoons white vinegar, 4 tablespoons sugar, 1 1/2 tablespoons water

(II) 1/2 teaspoon MSG, 1 1/2 tablespoons soy sauce, 1/2 tablespoon sugar, 1/2 teaspoon five-spice powder, 1 cup water

Method:

1. Put ingredients (I) in a small saucepan. Melt the sugar over a low flame. Pour slowly into the cooked rice. (Stir the rice loose with chopsticks first.) Keep stirring as you add the solvent of ingredients (I).

2. Bake the laver over a low flame for a few seconds. Put fried bean curds in ingredients (II). Let boil for 5 minutes. Remove and squeeze dry. Rub them gently and carefully to make a hole in the middle of each one. Cut each one across to make 2 triangles. Remove the soft inner part.

3. Spread rice thinly on the laver. Put egg shreds, ginger shreds, cucumber shreds, and pork fluff on top. Shape them into a long strip. Use a bamboo mat to roll it up (or use your hands). Cut into 1" sections. Serve.

4. If you use fried bean curds, stuff each triangle with rice. Sprinkle sesame seeds, egg shreds, and ginger shreds on top. Serve.

Note:

Raw fish slices, cooked squid shreds, fried pork or beef shreds, caviar, jam, cheese, and various kinds of sauce can all be used as filling.

台式香菇肉粽

Black Mushroom and Pork Tsung-Tzu, Taiwanese Style

Ingredients:

21 ounces glutinous rice, 10 ounces pork belly, 8-10 dried black mushrooms, 4 tablespoons dried baby shrimps, 4-5 ounces peanuts, 4 tablespoons lard or oil, 5 talbespoons minced red scallion head, 2/3 cup water or soup stock

(I) 1 1/2 tablespoons soy sauce, 1/2 teaspoon black pepper, 1/2 teaspoon salt, 1/2 teaspoon MSG

Method:

1. Wash the rice. Drain. Cut the pork into large cubes. Soak the dried black mushrooms in water. Remove footstalks. Dice. Soak dried baby shrimps in water for a while. Wash the peanuts. Soak in water overnight. Wash again on the second day.
2. Put oil in a frying pan. Fry minced red scallion head for a while. Add pork cubes, diced black mushroom, and dried baby shrimps. Stir-fry till the color of the pork changes. Add ingredients (I). Mix well. Remove, leaving oil in the pan.
3. Put rice and peanuts in the pan. Stir-fry over a low to medium flame. Add water or soup stock little by little during the frying. Fry till the rice looks transparent and sticky.
4. Use brown, spotted bamboo leaves. Fold one-third of the leaf up to make a spoon shape. Spread 1 1/2 tablespoons of fried rice in it. Put 1 tablespoon of filling on top. Cover with 1 1/2 tablespoons of fried rice. Wrap it according to the steps in Tsung-Tzu, Hu-Chow Style. (but Taiwan tsung-tzu is shorter than Hu-chow tsung-tzu).
5. Steam over a high flame for 1-1 1/2 hours. Serve.

Note:

Long glutinous rice is not as sticky as round glutinous rice.

筒仔米糕　　油飯

Mi-Kao (Rice Cake); Yiu-Fen (Oiled Rice)

Ingredients:

3 cups glutinous rice, 2 teaspoons rock sugar, 3 tablespoons oil, 6 tablespoons minced red scallion head, 1/3 cup soup stock,

(I) 13 ounces pork belly, dried black mushrooms, 4 tablespoons dried baby shrimps, 10 dried or fresh marrons

(II) 1/2 teaspoon salt, 1/2 teaspoon MSG

Method:

1. Wash the rice. Cook in boiling water for 5-8 minutes. Remove and drain.
2. Cut pork into 1"-wide slices. Soak dried black mushrooms in water for 2 hours. Remove footstalks. Cut into wide strips. Soak dried baby shrimps in water for 5 minutes. Soak marrons in water for 4 hours. Remove the skin. Put in a bowl with rock sugar and fill with water. Steam for 40 minutes.
3. Put oil in a frying pan. Fry the minced red scallion head for a few seconds. Add ingredients (I) and (II). Stir-fry till the color of the pork changes. Remove. Leave the juice in the pan.
4. Put the rice in the pan. Stir-fry over a low to medium flame. Add soup stock little by little during frying. put the stir-fried mixture in when the rice is cooked. Mix well. This is the so-called yiu-fan (oiled rice).
5. Mi-kao is made by spreading a layer of the fried mixture on the bottom of a rice bowl or container, covering with fried rice, and steaming over a high flame for 20-30 minutes. Pour it out upside down. Serve.

Note:

Mi-kao can be cooked only with pork. Sauce or parsley can be added when serving to make it more delicious.

廣東粥

Congee, Cantonese Style

Ingredients:

1-2 yiu-tiao, 1 cup round glutinous rice, 2-3 scallions or parsley sprigs, pepper

(I) 1 salted duck egg, 1 thousand-year egg, 10 ounces ground pork or 1 large pork bone

Method:

1. Mince yiu-tiao and scallions or parsley. Shell the eggs. Crush them by hand. Wrap the ground pork with a piece of cloth. (If you use a pork bone, there is no need to wrap it.)
2. Wash the rice. Bring to a boil with ingredients (I) in a pot. Lower the heat after it comes to a boil. Simmer till most of the rice is no longer in whole grains. Remove the pork.
3. Put minced yiu-tiao in a bowl. Pour in the congee. Sprinkle minced scallion or parsley and pepper on top. Serve.

Notes:

1. If you serve the congee by pouring it on very thinly sliced raw fish, it is called yu-sheng (raw-fish) congee.
2. Beef slices or pork liver slices can be cooked in the congee.

芋香鹹粥

Taro Congee

Ingredients:

1 cup round glutinous rice or 3 cups cooked rice, 1/2 taro, 2 tablespoons scrap, 6 tablespoons dried baby shrimps or small dried fish, 3 tablespoons oil, 4 tablespoons minced red scallion head, 5 ounces ground pork

(I) 2 teaspoons salt, 1/2 teaspoon MSG, 1/2 teaspoon pepper, 11/2 tablespoons minced parsley

Method:

1. Wash the round glutinous rice. Simmer with 30 cups of water to make congee. If you use cooked rice, just simmer it with 6 cups of water to make congee.
2. Peel the taro. Cut into large cubes. Fry till golden brown. Remove and drain. Chop the scrap. Wash the dried baby shrimps or small dried fish. Drain.
3. Put oil in a frying pan. Stir-fry the minced red scallion and dried baby shrimps first. Add congee, ingredients (I), and other ingredients. Bring to a boil. Let boil till taro is very soft.

臘八粥
La-Ba Congee

Ingredients:

1 cup round glutinous rice, $1/4$ cup black dates, $1/4$ cup lotus seeds, $1/4$ cup red beans, $1/4$ cup green beans, $1/4$ cup peanuts, $1/4$ cup lily bulbs, $1/4$ cup pine seeds, $1/4$ cup dried longan, 1 cup sugar or rock sugar, $1/4$ cup white gourd sugar

Method:

1. Wash the rice. Soak the above ingredients except longan, sugar, and white gourd sugar in water for 4 hours.
2. Put all ingredients except the sugar in a saucepan with water. Bring to a boil. Lower the flame and simmer till all ingredients turn very tender. Add sugar. Serve.

八珍鹹粥
Salted Ba-Jen Congee
(Salted Congee with Eight Ingredients)

Ingredients:

$1^1/2$ cups round glutinous rice, about 30 cups water, 1 chicken liver, 1 chicken gizzard, 5 ounces cowpeas, 5 ounces fresh oysters, 1 tablespoon cornstarch, 1 sea cucumber, 2 tablespoons very small dried baby shrimps, 2 tablespoons minced ham, $1/2$ teaspoon pepper

(I) 2 teaspoons salt, $1/2$ teaspoon MSG, $1/2$ tablespoon ginger juice

Method:

1. Wash the rice. Add water and bring to a boil. Lower the flame and simmer till most of the rice is no longer in whole grains.
2. Wash the chicken liver and gizzard and cowpeas. Dice. Cook in boiling water for a while. Wash the oysters. Drain. Mix with cornstarch. Cook in boiling water for 1 minute. Remove the intestinal organs from the sea cucumber. Dice. Cook in boiling water for 5 minutes. After boiling the above ingredients, soak them in cold water.
3. Put all these ingredients and ingredients (I) in the congee. Let boil for 5 minutes. Sprinkle some pepper on top. Serve.

八寶飯
Ba-Bao Rice

Ingredients:

2 cups round glutinous rice, $1/4$ cup rock sugar, $1^2/3$ cups water, $1/2$ cup lotus seeds, $1/2$ cup gingkos, $1/2$ cup sweet peas, $1/2$ cup black dates, 6 tablespoons lard, $1/2$ cup green and red papaya shreds, $1/2$ cup dried longans, $1/2$ cup raisins, $1/2$ cup sweet preserves

(I) $1/3$ teaspoon sweet osmanthus sauce, $1^1/2$ cups water, 1 tablespoon cornstarch

Method:

1. Wash the rice. Put the rice, rock sugar, and water in an electric rice cooker. Steam. Blend with lard while still hot.
2. Soak lotus seeds, gingkos, sweet peas, and black dates in water for 2 hours.
3. Brush a layer of lard all over the inside of a large soup bowl. Arrange lotus seeds, gingkos, papaya shreds, etc., on the bottom to make a pattern. Spread 1/2 cup of cooked rice evenly on top. Put red bean mash in the middle. Cover with the remaining cooked rice. Pour a tablespoon of lard on top. Put in a steamer. Steam for 40 minutes. Remove. Unmold upside down into a plate.
4. Bring ingredients (I) to a boil. Pour over Ba-Bao Rice. Serve.

甜米糕
Sweet Mi-Kao (Sweet Rice Cake)

Ingredients:

3 cups round glutinous rice, $1/2$ cup brown sugar, $2^1/2$ cups water, 6 tablespoons lard, $1/2$ teaspoon sweet osmanthus sauce, 3 tablespoons raisins

Method:

1. Wash the rice. Mix with brown sugar. Put in an electric cooker. Steam. Add lard and osmanthus sauce while still hot. Blend well.
2. Put the cooked rice in square mold. Press the rice to make it even. Sprinkle raisins on top. Let stand. Cut into pieces when cold.

碗粿
Rice Pudding in Bowl

Ingredients:

6 cups boiling water, 21 ounces rice powder, 10 ounces pork belly, 4 tablespoons dried baby shrimps, several dried black mushrooms, 1 tablespoon lard or oil, 4 tablespoons oil, 4 tablespoons minced red scallion head

(I) 3 tablespoons soy sauce, 1/2 tablespoon rock sugar, 1/2 teaspoon salt, 1/2 teaspoon MSG, 1/2 tablespoon ginger wine, 2/3 teaspoon pepper

Method:

1. Add boiling water to the rice powder little by little. Stir well to make a thick paste.
2. Dice the pork belly. Soak dried baby shrimps in water for 10 minutes. Dice. Reserve the water used to soak the shrimps. Remove footstalks from the dried balck mushrooms. Soak in water for 2 hours. Dice. Brush lard or oil evenly on the inside of 6-8 Chinese rice bowls.
3. Put oil in a frying pan. Fry the minced red scallion head till browned. Add all dice and ingredients (I). Stir-fry till done.
4. Pour rice paste into each bowl. (Fill 70%-80% of each bowl.) Spread the cooked dice evenly on top of each bowl.
5. Put in a steamer. Steam for 15-20 minutes. Open the cover once in a while to let out some hot air during steaming, or it will look ugly after it is cooked.

Note:

Shrimps or fish slices can be used to replace the pork. You can also make sweet rice pudding by mixing rice powder with brown sugar syrup.

發糕
Leavened Rice Cake

Ingredients:

21 ounces rice powder, 5 ounces cake flour, 1/2 tablespoon baking soda, 2/3 cup sugar or brown sugar, 3 cups water

Method:

1. Mix rice powder, flour, and baking soda. Sift. Mix sugar with water. Stir until the sugar melts. Pour in the mixed powder to make a paste. Let stand for 15 minutes.
2. Pour the paste into rice bowls. Fill about 70% of each bowl. You can also use paper molds to make different patterns.
3. Put in a steamer. Steam over a high flame for 15 minutes.

Notes:

1. To make salted leavened rice cake, you can use smoked pork cubes and dried baby shrimps instead of sugar.
2. Cocoa or cherry juice can be added when making sweet leavened rice cake.
3. Do not make the paste too thin. The paste is thick enough when it is hard to stir it with a chopstick.

江西辣味米粉

Hot Rice Noodles, Chiang-Hsi Style

Ingredients:

1 pack of Chiang-Hsi rice noodles, 1/2 cabbage, 1/2 cup shredded pork, 2 tablespoons small dried fish, several chili peppers, 6 tablespoons oil, 2/3 cup soup stock or water

(I) 1/2 tablespoon soy sauce, 1/4 teaspoon five-spice powder, 1 teaspoon cornstarch, 1/3 tablespoon wine

(II) 1 1/2 teaspoons salt, 1/2 teaspoon MSG

Method:

1. Soak rice noodles in hot water for 20 minutes. Stir them lose by hand.
2. Remove old leaves from the cabbage. Wash clean. Cut into wide shreds. Marinate the pork shreds with ingredients (I) for 10 minutes. Wash the small dried fish. Drain. Cut the chili peppers into wide shreds.
3. Put oil in a frying pan. Fry the small dried fish and chili pepper shreds first for a few seconds. Add the pork shreds. Stir-fry till the color of the pork changes. Add soup stock or water and cabbage. Stir-fry over a high flame till the cabbage turns soft. Put the rice noodles and ingredients (II) in. Mix well. Cover the pan and simmer for 3-5 minutes. Uncover and stir-fry for a short while. Serve.

台式炒米粉

Stir-Fried Rice Noodles, Taiwanese Style

Ingredients:

1/3 cup shredded pork, some leeks, 5 ounces bean sprouts, 2 tablespoons scrap, 1 pack of thin rice noodles, 6 tablespoons oil, 4 tablespoons minced red scallion head, 1/2 cup soup stock

(I) 1/3 tablespoon soy sauce, 2 teaspoons cornstarch, 1/3 tablespoon ginger wine

(II) 1 teaspoon salt, 1/2 teaspoon MSG, 1 1/2 tablespoons soy sauce

Method:

1. Marinate shredded pork with ingredients (I) for 20 minutes.
2. Wash the leeks. Cut into 1" sections. Remove the root parts from the bean sprouts. Wash clean. Chop the scrap. Soak rice noodles for a short while in water. Remove and drain.
3. Put oil in a frying pan. Fry the minced scallion head for a few seconds. Stir-fry the shredded pork for a while. Add the chopped scrap, bean sprouts, soup stock, rice noodles, and ingredients (II). Stir-fry over a high flame. Add leeks when there is no more juice left. Stir-fry for a short while. Serve.

鹹味米台目
Salted Mi-Tai-Mu

Ingredients:

10 ounces green-stemmed flat cabbage, 8 ounces lean shredded pork, 4 tablespoons oil, 1/2 tablespoon chopped garlic, 3 tablespoons small dried fish, 8 cups soup stock, 2 1/2 pounds mi-tai-mu

(I) 2 tablespoons soy sauce, 2 teaspoons ginger wine

(II) 1 1/2 teaspoons salt, 1/2 teaspoon MSG

Method:

1. Wash the green-stemmed flat cabbage. Cut into long strips. Marinate the shredded pork with ingredients (I) for 10 minutes.
2. Put oil in a frying pan. Fry the chopped garlic and small dried fish till they smell good. Add the pork shreds. Stir fry till the color of the pork changes. Add the soup stock, mi-tai-mu, and ingredients (II). Bring to a boil. Put in the green-stemmed flat cabbage. Let boil for 1 1/2 fminutes. Serve.

Note:

Mi-Tai-mu is a kind of noodles made from rice powder. It is fresh and wet. Rice noodles are usually dried and can be preserved for a long time.

什錦米台目冰
Mi-Tai-Mu and Assorted Ingredients with Chopped Ice

Ingredients:

1/2 cup sugar, 6 cups water, 21 ounces mi-tai-mu, 3 tablespoons fen-yuan, 3 tablespoons yu-yuan, 3 tablespoons kuo-yuan, 2 cups chopped ice

Method:

Melt sugar in water. (Bring the water to a boil first.) Let cool. Add all the other ingredients. Serve.

Note:

You can buy already-cooked fen-yuan, yu-yuan, and kuo-yuan. Fen-yuan are the small balls made from cornstarch or potato powder, very tender when cooked. yu-yuan are the small balls made from taro powder and potato powder, The color is light purple. Kuo-yuan are made from rice powder. Their color is light yellow.

糖年糕
Sweet Nien-Kao (Year Cake)

Ingredients:

6-7 cups water, 21 ounces brown sugar, 10 black dates, 32 ounces glutinous rice powder, 10 ounces tsai-lai rice powder, 8 tablespoons lard

Method:

1. Put water in a small saucepan. Add the sugar. Bring to a boil to melt the sugar. Wash the dates. Soak in water for 4 hours.
2. Mix rice powders together. Pour sugar syrup into the powder little by little, stirring till it is well mixed. Add 6 tablespoons of lard. Blend well.
3. Put a piece of cellophane in a steamer. (Brush a layer of oil on the cellophane first.) Pour the thick paste on the cellophane. Garnish with dates on top. Steam over a high flame for 2-4 hours. (The water in the steamer should be boiling before you pour in the paste.)

Notes:

1. You can stick a chopstick into nien-kao; if no juice sticks to the chopstick, nien-kao is fully cooked.
2. Put enough water in the steamer. If you add water during the steaming, nien-kao will not taste good.
3. Nien-Kao is more elastic if tsai-lai rice powder is used. If you like sticky nien-kao, do not add adny tsai-lai rice powder; use glutinous rice powder only.

廣式蘿蔔糕
Turnip Cake, Cantonese Style

Ingredients:

6 tablespoons lard, 1/3 cup chopped dried baby shrimps, 4 pounds white turnip, 3 teaspoons salt, 1-1 1/2 cups water, 21 ounces tsai-lai rice powder, 1 tablespoon chopped parsley

(I) 1/3 cup chopped smoked pork, 1/3 cup chopped smoked sausage, 1 1/2 teaspoons white pepper, 1 tablespoon sugar, 1/2 teaspoon MSG

Method:

1. Put oil in a frying pan. Heat for a while. Fry the chopped dried baby shrimps till they smell good. Add turnip shreds and salt. Let the mixture boil till it turns pastelike. Add ingredients (I). Mix well. Turn off the heat.
2. Add water to tsai-lai rice powder to make a thick paste. Mix with the turnip paste.
3. Brush oil on a piece of cellophane. Put it in a steamer. Pour the mixed paste on the cellophane. Steam over a high flame for 2 hours. Remove. Put it in a windy place to cool down. Sprinkle chopped parsley on top when it is cold. Slice. Serve. you can also grill the slices, then serve.

Notes:

1. The chopped smoked pork and sausage should be 1/4" cubes.
2. Use juicy turnips with a thin skin.
3. Stick a chopstick into the turnip cake to check on whether it is cooked.

煎年糕

Grilled Nien-Kao

Ingredients:

6 tablespoons oil, 2 tablespoons water, minced parsley, 21 ounces nien-kao

Dipping (I):

1 tablespoon minced garlic, 3 tablespoons soy sauce, 1/2 tablespoon chili peper sauce

Dipping (II):

2 tablespoons sweet and hot sauce, 1 tablespoon thick soy sauce, 1 tablespoon seafood sauce

Method:

1. Mix ingredients in dipping (I) together. Put 2 tablespoons of oil in a frying pan. Put dipping (II) and the water in. Let boil for 1 minute. Sprinkle minced parsley on top.

2. Put oil in a clean frying pan. Array nien-kao slices in the pan. Grill over medium heat till both sides are browned. Remove. Dip in the two dressing to eat.

Note:

It is very delicious to wrap jam or sauce with grilled nien-kao.

素炒年糕

Stir-Fried Nien-kao with Vegetable

Ingredients:

26 ounces nien-kao, 20 dried black mushrooms, 10 ounces green-stemmed flat cabbage, 4 tablespoons oil, 3 tablespoons soy sauce, 1/2 tablespoon sugar, 1/2 cup soup stock, 1/2 teaspoon salt, 1/2 teaspon MSG, sesame oil.

Method:

1. Slice nien-kao on a slant. Remove footstalks from black mushrooms. Soak in water for 2 hours. Wash vegetable clean. Cut into 1" sections.

2. Put oil in a frying pan. Stir-fry the black mushrooms for a while. Add soy sauce, sugar, and soup stock. Cover the pan. Boil for 1-2 minutes. Put nien-kao, the vegetable, and other ingredients in the pan. Stir-fry till the vegetable turns soft. Serve.

桂花酒釀湯圓

Tang-Yuan (Balls of Glutinous Rice) in Osmanthus and Fermented Rice Soup

炸糯米丸子

Fried Glutinous Rice Balls

Ingredients:

1-2 cups water, 21 ounces glutinous rice powder, 1 cup red bean mash, 1 cup sesame powder, 1/3 cup sugar, lard

(I) $1^1/_2$ tablespoons sweet fermented rice, $^1/_4$ teaspoon osmanthus sauce, 1 egg, $1^1/_2$ tablespoons sugar (for one serving)

Method:

1. Add some water to 3-4 tablespoons of rice powder to make a dough. Put in a small saucepan of boiling water. Let boil till cooked. Ladle out. Put into rice powder. Add water. Knead to dough. This dough is made for wrapping.

2. A. Red bean mash filling: See Red Bean Pancakes for how to prepare red bean mash.

   B. Sesame filling: Mix sesame powder, sugar, and lard together to make dough. Divide into small pieces. Rub each into a $^3/_4$"-diameter ball. The sesame balls are used as filling.

3. Wrap filling with wrappers made from the glutinous rice powder dough. You can shape it to the patterns you like. Tang-yuan can also be made by putting the wet filling balls in dry glutinous rice powder in a large tray. Shake the tray to let rice powder coat the filling heavily. This is called shou-yiao-tang-yuan—tang-yuan made by hands and shaking.

4. Bring a saucepan of water to a boil. Put in tang-yuan (also called yuan-hsiao). Remember to stir once in a while to keep the tang-yuan from sticking to the bottom of the pan. Simmer over a low to medium flame for 3 minutes. Raise the flame to high. Let boil till the tang-yuan are floating. Ladle out.

5. Bring ingredients (I) to a boil with a cup of water. Put in the cooked tang-yuan. This is the Tang-Yuan in Osmanthus and Fermented Rice Soup.

6. Put some artificial color in the rice powder, then make it into small balls. These balls are called yuan-tzu. Yuan-tzu can be served salted or sweet.

7. Besides boiling, both tang-yuan and yuan-tzu can be coated with flour, then fried in over-medium-hot oil till scorched. Drain and serve. Dip in honey, sugar, or sweet sauce to eat.

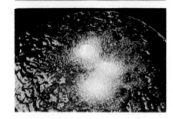

鮮肉湯圓　　圓仔湯

Pork Tang-Yuan　　Yuan-Tzu Soup

Ingredients:
7-8 ounces lean ground pork, 10 ounces spinach or tung-hao, 26 ounces dough of glutinous rice powder, 8 cups clear soup stock

(I)　1 teaspoon salt, 1/2 teaspoon MSG, 1/3 teaspoon pepper, 1/2 tablespoon ginger wine

(II)　1 teaspoon salt, 1/2 teaspoon MSG, some sesame oil

Method:
1. Mix ground pork with ingredients (I). Wash the vegetable. Cut into 1" sections.
2. Divide the dough into 1 ounce small balls. Press into a round wrapper with your hands. Put 1/2 tablespoon of pork filling in each wrapper.
3. Bring clear soup stock to a boil. Put in tang-yuan. Let boil till tang-yuan are floating. Add the vegetable. Let boil for 1 1/2 minutes. Add ingredients (II). Serve.

Note:
This is the method for making Pork Tang-Yuan. Yuan-Tzu is small Tang-Yuan without stuffing. To make Yuan-Tzu Soup, just follow step 3.

魷魚羹

Squid Broth

Ingredients:

13 ounces fish paste, 1 large soaked squid, 6 cups clear soup stock, 3 tablespoons stock fish, 3 tablespoons bamboo shoot shreds, 3 tablespoons fungus shreds, 3 tablespoons carrot shreds, 3 tablespoons shredded pork, 4 tablespoons cornstarch paste, 2 tablespoons choopped parsley

(I) ¹/₂ tablespoon ginger wine, 2 tablespoons chopped celery, ¹/₂ teaspoon salt, 1 teaspoon sugar, ¹/₂ teaspoon pepper

(II) 1 teaspoon salt, ¹/₂ tablespoon soy sauce, ¹/₂ teaspoon MSG

(III) 3 teaspoons sesame oil, 2 tablespoons black vinegar

Method:

1. Blend the fish paste well with ingredients (I). Cut the squid into wide strips. Wipe them dry. Put in the fish paste. Blend well.
2. Put tablespoon after tablespoon of fish paste in a saucepan of boiling water. Let boil till all the pieces turn hard and are floating. Ladle out.
3. Bring clear soup stock, stock fish, and ingredients (II) to a boil. Let boil for 3 minutes. Put in all kinds of shreds and the fish-paste-coated squid. Bring to a boil. Keep boiling for 1 to 2 minutes. Add cornstarch paste to make the soup thick. Remove. Add ingredients (III) and chopped parsley. Serve.

Note:

Pork broth can also be cooked according to above steps. Use fish-paste-coated pork instead.

炸蚵餅

Fried Oyster Patty

Ingredients:

10 ounces fresh oyster, ¹/₂ tablespoon cornstarch, 21 ounces leeks, ¹/₄ cup chopped cabbage, 5 ounces lean ground pork, 2 cups all-purpose flour, ²/₃ teaspoon salt, a pan of oil for frying

(I) ¹/₂ teaspon salt, ¹/₂ teaspoon MSG, ¹/₂ teaspoon pepper

(II) 1 tablespoon chopped garlic, 3 tablespoons soy sauce, 1 tablespoon sweet and hot sauce

Method:

1. Wash the oysters. Drain. Blend with cornstarch.
2. Wash the leeks. Dice. Mix the chopped leeks and cabbage with the oysters, pork, and ingredients (I) to make filling.
3. Make a thick paste by mixing flour, salt, and some water.
4. Put about 1 tablespoon of the flour batter in a large ladle. Put 3 tablespoons of filling on top. Put a layer of flour paste on top to cover the filling.
5. Heat oil for frying to very hot. Put in the ladle. Fry for 5 minutes. The patty will look scorched by then. Tip the patty out carefully. Fry for a short while. Ladle out. Drain. Dip in ingredients (II) to eat.

Note:

You can choose the ingredients you like to make filling.

糖蕃薯

Sweet Potato in Sugar Syrup

Ingredients:

2¹/₂ pounds sweet potatoes

(I) 10 ounces brown sugar, 4 ounces sugar, 2 tablespoons malt sugar or 2-3 tablespoons rock sugar, ¹/₂ cup water, 3 tablespoons oil

Method:

1. Peel the sweet potatoes. Cut into pieces 2" wide and 3" long. Wash clean. Drain.
2. Put ingredients (I) in a saucepan. Bring to a boil. When the sugar is melted, add the sweet potatoes. Simmer over a low flame till they look transparent and shiny. Serve.

Notes:

1. Bananas, pineapples, apples, pears, etc., can all be cooked this way. If the fruit you use is sour, add more sugar.
2. When boiling, do not stir it too hard, or you will mash the sweet potatoes.
3. Sweet potato can also be cooked by coating with flour paste, then frying.

海鮮捲

Seafood Rolls

Ingredients:

6-8 pieces of wet bean curd skin, 2 tablespoons flour, 2 tablespoons water, 13-21 ounces fresh oysters (shelled), 10 ounces bean sprouts, 3-5 tablespoons pork cubes, 3-5 tablespoons chopped celery, ¹/₂ teaspoon salt, ¹/₂ teaspoon MSG, ¹/₂ teaspoon xanthoxylum seed powder, a pan 'of oil for frying, 2 tablespoons oil, ¹/₂ tablespoon chopped garlic

(I) 1 tablespoon seafood sauce, 3 tablespoons ketchup, 2 tablespoons sugar, 2 tablespoons vinegar, ¹/₂ teaspoon MSG, 2 teaspoons cornstarch, 4 tablespoons water

Method:

1. Cut each bean curd skin into 2 or 3 parts. Mix flour with water to make a thick paste.
2. Wash the oysters. Drain. Wash the bean sprouts. Drain. Mix the oysters, bean sprouts, pork cubes, chopped celery, salt, MSG, and xanthoxylum seed powder to make filling.
3. Wrap 2 tablespoons of filling with a piece of bean curd skin. Shape it into a long roll. Seal the roll with flour paste. Put in over-medium-hot oil. Fry till scorched. Ladle out. Drain.
4. Put 2 tablespoons of oil in a frying pan. Fry the chopped garlic till it smells good. Add ingredients (I). Bring to a boil. Pour it on the fried seafood rolls. Serve.

Notes:

1. Shelled shrimps can be used as filling.
2. Fry the roll immediately after you make it. Remember to turn each roll from side to side during frying. Keep the flame over-medium-high.
3. Spring roll skin can be used to replace bean curd skin, but rolls wrapped with spring roll skin have to be fried twice. Frist, fry them in over-medium-hot oil for 7-8 minutes. Then heat the oil to boiling hot, put the rolls back in, and fry for 1-2 minutes.

油豆腐細粉

Yiu-Tou-Fu (Fried Bean Curd) and Bean Threads Soup

Ingredients:
2 bundles of bean threads, 6-8 cups soup stock, 4 tablespoons chopped celery, $1/2$ tablespoon sesame oil
(I) 4 pork-stuffed yiu-tou-fu, 4 pork-stuffed rolls of bean curd skin, 4 egg dumplings or some fish balls
(II) 4 tablespoons salted vegetable root shreds, 2 teaspoons salt, $1/2$ teaspoon MSG
Method:
1. Soak bean threads in water for 30 minutes. Cut into long sections.
2. Bring ingredients (I) and soup stock to a boil for about 10 minutes. Put bean threads in. Let boil for 1 minute. Add ingredients (II). Bring to a boil. Serve.
3. Sprinkle on some chopped celery and sesame oil before eating.

炸龍鳳腿

Fried Lumg-Fang-Tuei

Ingredients:
10 ounces pork belly, 8 ounces chicken breast, 5 ounces water chestnuts, 1 piece of chu-wang-yiu, 3 tablespoons oil, 2 tablespoons chopped celery, 10 ounces cabbage (chopped), $1/4$ cup carrot shreds, 1 cups flour paste, 1 pan of oil for frying
(I) 2 teaspoons salt, 1 tablespoon sugar, $1/2$ teaspoon five-spice powder, $1/2$ tablespoon cornstarch, $1/2$ teaspoon MSG
(II) 3 tablespoons chili pepper sauce, 3 tablespoons ketchup

Method:
1. Chop the pork belly. Shred the chicken breast. Chop the water chestnuts. Cut the chu-wang-yiu into 4"×4" squares.
2. Put 3 tablespoons of oil in a frying pan. Stir-fry the chopped celery, chopped pork, chicken shreds, chopped water chestnuts, chopped cabbage, carrot shreds, and ingredients (I). Keep stir-frying till the color of the pork changes. Remove. This mixture is the filling.
3. Wrap 2-3 tablespoons of filling with a piece of chu-wang-yiu. Form it into the shape of a chicken leg. Seal with flour paste.

4. Heat oil for frying to over-medium-hot. Fry lung-fang-tuei for about 7-10 minutes. (Coat each one with a layer of flour paste first.) Ladle out. Dip in the mixed ingredients (II) to eat.
Notes:
1. Fish paste, bean ~routs, bean curds, peanut powder, etc., can all be used as filling. If there is too much juice, add some cornstarch or pour off the juice.
2. The flour paste is make by mixing 3-4 eggs, 3/4 cup flour, $1/2$ tablespoon oil, $1/2$ teaspoon salt, and some water.

麻辣粉皮湯

Hot and Spicy Fen-Pi Soup

Ingredients:

21 ounces fen-pi (fen-pi is a kind of wide noodles made from green beans), 10 ounces pig's blood curds, 3 ounces leeks, 4 tablespoons oil, 2 tablespoons ground chili pepper, 1 tablespoon xanthoxylum seed powder, 5 ounces ground pork, 8 cups soup stock or water.

(I) 2 teaspoons salt, 2 tablespoons chili oil, 3 tablespoons fried chopped preserved vegetable, 1/2 teaspoon MSG

Method:

1. Wash fen-pi and pig's blood curds. Cut them into wide strips. Wash the leeks. Dice.
2. Put oil in frying pan. Fry the ground chili pepper and xanthoxylum seed powder for a while. Add the ground pork. Stir-fry till the color of the pork changes. Add soup stock, fen-pi, and pig's blood curds. Let boil for 3 minutes. Add ingredients (I) and leek dice. Serve.

Notes:

1. This is a good dish in wintertime, for it is very spicy and hot. Having it in summertime can help you to sweat so that you will feel good as you cool off afterward.
2. It is suggested that cornstarch be added in wintertime.

拌涼粉

Cold-Blended Liang-Fen

Ingredients:

1 tablespoon oil. 21 ounces liang-fen (liang-fen looks like gelatin; it is half transparent and is made from green beans)

(I) 4-5 tablespoons ground pork, 2 tablespoons hot bean sauce, 1 1/2 tablespoons soy sauce, 1/2 teaspoon salt, 1 tablespoon sugar, 1 tablespoon wine, 3 tablespoons water

(II) 2 1/2 tablespoons chopped salted vegetable root, 2 tablespoons chopped spiced bean curd, 3 tablespoons chopped scallion, 2-3 tablespoons chopped garlic, 4 tablespoons chili oil, 1/2 teaspoon MSG

Method:

1. Put oil in a frying pan. Stir-fry ingredients (I) for 3 minutes. Remove.
2. Cut the liang-fen into wide strips. Pour the stir-fried ingredients (I) and the well-mixed ingredients (II) on top. Serve. Blend all ingredients well before eating.

Notes:

1. Though this is a cold-blended dish, do not put it in the refrigerator. Liang-fen will be no longer elastic after refrigeration.
2. Liang-fen can also be as ingredient in soup.

花生湯
Peanut Soup

Ingredients:

13 ounces peanuts, 15-20 cups water

(I) $1/2$ cup rock sugar, 1 slice of old ginger

Method:

1. Wash the peanuts.
2. Bring the water to a boil. Add the peanuts and ingredients (I). Return to a boil, lower the flame, and simmer for 1 hour. Try some peanuts, If they are very soft, serve. If not, keep simmering for a while.

Notes:

1. Black dates, dried longan meat, red beans, etc., can also be added.
2. You can also add $1^1/2$ teaspoons soda powder. The peanuts will be easier to cook this way.

炸芝麻薯球
Fried Sesame Balls

Ingredients:

1 red-fleshed sweet potato (about 5 ounces), 8 ounces yuan-hsiao powder, 1 tablespoon sugar, some 140°F water, $1/2$ cup sesame seeds, a pan of oil for frying

Method:

1. Peel the sweet potato. Cut into small pieces. Steam till cooked. Mash it while still hot. Mix with yuan-hsiao powder, sugar, and hot water to make a dough. Knead till it is smooth and shining. Divide into several small balls. Put a layer of sesame seeds on top of each one.
2. Put in over-medium-hot oil. Fry over medium flame. Keep stirring with a spatula during frying. After 1-2 minutes, press each ball with the spatula. The balls will expand to 2-3 times their size. Ladle out when they are browned on the surface. Serve.

Notes:

1. You can stuff the balls with filling, then fry.
2. Yuan-hsiao powder is added to prevent the balls from splitting open while expanding.

春餅二式

Chun-Bing (Spring Rolls), Two Different Styles

Ingredients:
10 ounces tender leeks, 3 tablespoons oil, 10 ounces lean pork or beef (shredded), 3-4 tablespoons shredded bamboo shoot, 4 tablespoons shredded dried black mushrooms, 3 tablespoons cornstarch paste, 26 ounces chun-bing-pi (spring roll skins), 1 pan of oil for frying
(I) 2 tablespoons flour, $2^1/2$ tablespoons water
(II) 1 tablespoon seafood sauce, $1^1/2$ teaspoons salt, 2 teaspoons sugar, $1/2$ teaspoon MSG, $1/2$ tablespoon wine, $1/2$ teaspoon pepper

Method:
1. Wash the tender leeks. Cut into 3"-long sections. Mix well with ingredients (I).
2. Put oil in a frying pan. Stir-fry all kinds of shreds and ingredients (II) over a high flame for 3 minutes. Add the leeks. Stir-fry for a short while. Add cornstarch paste to make it less juicy. Remove. This is the filling.
3. Wrap 2 tablespoons of filling with a piece of spring roll skin. Make rolls $2^3/4" \times 3/4"$. Serve. You can also seal the rolls with the paste made with ingredients (I), then put them in over-medium-hot oil and fry till browned. Ladle out. Drain and serve.

Notes:
1. You can use the ingredients you like to make filling.
2. If the filling is too juicy, add some cornstarch.

天婦羅

Tempura

Ingredients:
1 large turnip, 1 cup pig's blood cake, $1/2$ cup each of all kinds of tempura, $1/2$ cup fish balls
(I) 10 ounces spareribs, 2 tablespoons stock fish, 1 scallion, 1 slice of giner, 1 talbespoon wine, 12 cups water
(II) 3 tablespoons sweet and hot sauce, 3 tablespoons seafood sauce, 2 tablespoons oil, 2 tablespoons water

Method:
1. Peel the turnip. Cut into 1" sections. Cut the pig's blood cake into 1" squares. Cut large tempura into smaller pieces.
2. Bring ingredients (I) to a boil. Simmer for 30 minutes. Add all other ingredients and simmer till the turnip pieces turn very tender.
3. Bring ingredients (II) to a boil.
4. You can serve it in soup or dip in ingredients (II) to eat.

Note:
The tempura mentioned here are different from the tempura in Japanese restaurants. Chinese tempura are made by frying the paste of mashed fish and flour.

台式肉圓

Jou-Yuan (Pork-Stuffed Balls), Taiwanese Style

Ingredients:

10 ounces pork belly, 1 bamboo shoot, several dried black mushrooms, 5 ounces dried turnip shreds, 5 ounces shelled shrimps, 4 tablespoons oil, 8 cups boiling water, 31 ounces sweet potato powder, a pan of oil for frying.

(I) $1^1/_2$ teaspoons salt, 1 tablespoon cornstarch, $^1/_2$ tablespoon ginger wine, $^1/_2$ teaspoon pepper, $^1/_2$ teaspoon MSG, $^1/_2$ tablespoon soy sauce

(II) 4 tablespoons white sauce, 2 tablespoons sweet and hot sauce, 1 tablespoon garlic-flavored soy sauce

Method:

1. Dice the pork and the bamboo shoot. Soak dried black mushrooms in water for a while. Dice. Soak dried turnip shreds in water for a while. Squeeze dry. Wash shelled shrimps clean. Pick out intestinal cords. Drain.
2. Put 3 tablespoons of oil in a frying pan. Stir-fry all dice and ingredients (I) for 3-5 minutes. Remove. This is the filling.

3. Add 150°F water little by little to the sweet potato powder. Keep stirring while adding water till it is thick and pastelike. (It should be semitransparent.)
4. Brush oil inside rice bowls. Pour $2^1/_2$ tablespoons of the paste into each bowl. Put 2-3 tablespoons of filling and shrimps on top of the paste. Cover the filling with more paste.
5. Put in a steamer. Steam for about 10 minutes. Remove. Let stand for 1 while to cool down. Pour it out. Jou-yuan is made.
6. Heat oil for frying to over-medium-hot. Put the jou-yuan in oil. Keep the flame very low. Fry till the skin of jou-yuan turns hard. Remove. Dip in ingredients (II) to eat.

Notes:

1. See the note for Grilled Oyster Paste for how to prepare white sauce.
2. Cornstarch can also be used to make the skin. The skin made from sweet potato powder is very elastic. The skin made from cornstarch is very soft. The best way is to combine both of them. The proportion of sweet potato powder to cornstarch is 8:1.

蚵仔煎

Grilled Oyster Paste

Ingredients:

$^1/_2$ cup oil, 10 ounces fresh oysters (shelled), 4 eggs, 10 ounces vegetable

(I) 1 cup cornstarch, $2^1/_2$ cups water, 1 teaspoon salt, $^1/_2$ teaspoon MSG, $^1/_2$ teaspoon pepper

(II) 1/3 cup peanut powder, 3 tablespoons sweet and hot sauce, 3 tablespoons white sauce

Method:

1. Mix ingredients (I) to make cornstarch paste.
2. Heat a frying pan over a medium flame to over-medium-hot. Put in $1^1/_2$ tablespoons of oil. Let it run all over the pan. Put about $2^1/_2$ ounces of oysters in. Pour 6 tablespoons of cornstarch paste on top immediately. Break one egg. Put it beside the paste. Break the yolk. Add some vegetable. Add some more oil along the edge of the paste. Raise the flame to high.

3. When the color of the paste changes, cover the vegetable and egg with the paste. Cook for a short while. Turn it over. Cook for 1-2 minutes. Remove Repeat steps 2 and 3 three times to make another three servings.
4. Pour ingredients (II) on top. Serve.

Note:

Make white sauce by mixing a cup of soup stock, 3 tablespoons flour, $^1/_2$ teaspoon salt, and 1/3 teaspoon MSG together. Bring to a boil over a low to medium flame, stirring during boiling till it is pastelike.

炸芋粿
Fried Yu-Kuo (Taro Cake)

Ingredients:

1 tablespoon oil, 1 taro (around 8 ounces), 18 ounces tsai-lai rice powder, 3 ounces yuan-hsiao powder, 1 tablespoon lard, 1/2 tablespoon minced red scallion head, some 150°F water

(I) 1/2 tablespoon chili pepper sauce, 1 teaspoon chopped garlic, 2 tablespoons chopped scallion (white parts only), 1/3 tablespoon sugar, 1/3 teaspoon MSG, 3 tablespoons thick soy sauce, 1 tablespoon clear soup stock, 2 tablespoons oil

Method:

1. Put oil in a frying pan. Mix ingredients (I) well. Bring to a boil for 1-2 minutes. Remove.
2. Wash the taro. Peel. Dice into small cubes (around 1/4").
3. Mix rice powder, yuan-hsiao powder, and taro cubes together.
4. Put a tablespoon of oil in a clean pan. Fry the minced red scallion head for a while. Remove. Put into the mixed powder.
5. Add hot water to the mixed powder little by little. Keep stirring till it becomes very thick paste.
6. Brush lard on a piece of cellophane. Put the cellophane in a steamer. Pour the paste on the cellophane. Steam over a high flame for 1 to 2 hours. Remove. Slice while still hot. Serve. you can also let it get cold, slice it, and deep-fry in medium-hot oil for 20 minutes. Ladle out, drain, and serve.
7. Dip in ingredients (I) to eat.

炸芋條

Fried Taro Sticks

Ingredients:

1 large taro, a pan of oil for frying

(I) 3-5 tablespoons cornstarch, 3 tablespoons lard, 4-6 tablespoons sugar, 1/2 teaspoon salt

Method:

1. Peel the taro. Cut into large pieces. Steam till it gets tender.
2. Press the cooked taro with your hands to mash it. Mix with ingredients (I) to make dough.
3. Divide the dough into small pieces. Rub each piece into a long stick or ball.
4. Put oil in a pan. Heat to very hot. Fry the taro sticks till scorched. Ladle out, Drain. Serve.

Note:

You can make salted taro sticks by adding pepper and MSG and using only 1/2 tablespoon of sugar.

甜冷點心類

Cold Desserts

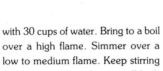

How to make gelatin and pudding

Picture 1
Agar and fish jelly are the major ingredients for making gelatin and pudding.
Pictures 2 and 3
Cut a strip of agar into 1" sections. Cut 6 pieces of fish jelly into 1" squares. Put them in a saucepan with 30 cups of water. Bring to a boil over a high flame. Simmer over a low to medium flame. Keep stirring during simmering. Simmer till both agar and fish jelly are melted.
Picture 4
Add 21 ounces sugar. Bring to a boil again.
Picture 5
Put a piece of gauze in a sieve. Strain the solution once. Let it stand for 1 hour. It will turn into jelly. This jelly can be used to make gelatin and/or pudding.

Notes:
1. If you use just agar to make jelly, the jelly will be very elastic.
2. Fish jelly is made from the air bladder of fish. If you use just fish jelly to make jelly, the jelly will be very soft and sticky.
3. Usually more agar is used in fruit gelatin; more fish jelly in pudding.

香蕉果凍
Banana Gelatin

Ingredients:

4-6 bananas, 1 large soup bowl of cold boiled water, $1/2$ teaspoon salt, 1 large soup bowl of jelly, $1/2$ cup fresh milk

Method:

1. Peel the bananas. Slice. Soak in salted cold boiled water.
2. Put half of the banana slices in a mold or large soup bowl. Arrange the slices to make a pattern. Pour on third of the jelly in. Wait for a while. Add half of the remaining jelly to the mold. Wait for another while. Pour all the remaining jelly in. Refrigerate.
3. When the gelatin is completely cold, unmold it upside down into a plate. Garnish with the reamining banana slices. Pour fresh milk on top. Serve.

Notes:

1. Banana slices should be kept in salted water, or they will turn black.
2. When adding the jelly to the mold, you can put the mold in cold water. It will help the jelly turn hard faster.
3. When you are waiting, remember to keep the jelly runny. It will be impossible to pour it into the mold if it has already set.
4. See p.115 for how to prepare jelly.

鳳梨果凍
Pineapple Gelatin

Ingredients:

1 can of pienapple slices, 1 large bowl of jelly (hot; sugar added)

Method:

1. Arrange pineapple slices in a large soup bowl to make a pattern.
2. Stir the hot jelly to cool it slightly. Pour part of it ino the bowl. Be careful, not to disturb the pattern made by the pineapple slices. Let stand for a while.
3. Pour in the remaining jelly. Put the bowl in the refrigerator.
4. When it has set, unmold it upside down on a plate. Pour pineapple juice on top. Serve.

Notes:

1. See "How to make gelatin and pudding" on p.115 for the method of preparing the jelly mentioned in the above two desserts.
2. You can garnish pineapple gelatin with diced fresh fruit.
3. Pineapple juice can be added when preparing the jelly.

鷄蛋布丁

Egg Pudding

Ingredients:

3 tablespoons cream, 6 eggs.

(I) ¹/₂ cup brown sugar, 4 to 6 tablespoons water

(II) 5 cups warm milk, 8 tablespoons fish jelly solvent, 8 tablespoons sugar

Method:

1. Bring ingredients (I) to a boil in a small saucepan. Stir clockwise with a chopstick during the boiling. Let it boil till it smells scorched. Drip some sugar syrup into cold water. If it turns to small balls immediately, the syrup is ready.
2. Coat the inside of 8 to 10 small molds with cream. Pour a tablespoon of syrup into each mold.
3. Beat the eggs and strain.
4. Bring ingredients (II) to a boil. Remove when there are bubbles. Add the egg batter and ¹/₂ tablespoon of cream when it is not too hot. Stir well. Pour into each mold. Put the molds in a 250°F oven. Bake for 15 to 20 minutes. (Or steam for 20 minutes.) Let cool, then refrigerate. Serve when it is completely cold.

Notes:

1. To prepare fish jelly solvent, boil 2¹/₂ pieces of fish jelly in 3 cups water. Simmer till 1¹/₂ cups of solvent are left. Strain. The solvent is ready.
2. If you choose steaming instead of baking, put the molds in the steamer after the water in the steamer is boiling. Steam over a low flame.

奶妯鷄蛋布丁

Creamy Egg Pudding

Ingredients:

6 slices of white bread, 6 eggs

(I) 3¹/₂ cups warm milk, 6 tablespoons fish jelly solvent, 8 tablespoons sugar, 1/3 teaspoon salt, 6 tablespoons cream

Method:

1. Cut the crusts off the bread. Soak in water for 2 hours. Rub with your hands to mash. Wrap in a piece of cheesecloth and squeeze dry.
2. Bring ingredients (I) to a boil over a low flame, stirring. Let it cool down a little bit.
3. Beat the eggs and strain. Pour in ingredients (I). Stir clockwise.
4. Was a large mold and wipe dry. Coat the inside with a layer of cream. Pour in the batter. Put in a steamer to steam for 30 minutes. Remember to open the steamer once every 5 minutes, or the pudding will look ugly. Unmold it onto a plate when it is done. Pour honey or fruit juice on top. Serve.